HEALING the HURTING HEART

JUNE HUNT

HARVEST HOUSE PUBLISHERS
Eugene, Oregon 97402

HEALING THE HURTING HEART

Eugene, Oregon 97402

Library of Congress Cataloging-in-Publication Data
Hunt, June
Healing the hurting heart / June Hunt.
p. cm.
ISBN 1-56507-362-2
1. Christian life—Dictionaries. 2. Christian life—Miscellanea. 3. Pastoral counseling—Dictionaries. 4. Pastoral counseling—Miscellanea. I. Title.
BV4488.H86 1995
248.4'03—dc20 95-13205
CIP

Printed in the United States of America.

To Nadine Saucier, my first mentor–

. . . who introduced me to the Savior and led me into a relationship with Him.

. . . who saw that I was a blank page spiritually and faithfully wrote God's truth on my heart.

. . . who welcomed me as a two-year "visitor" in her high school Bible class.

. . . who took my calls and answered all my questions through my college years.

. . . who was a human source of security until I could find my security in Jesus.

Contents

Part 5:
Anchored Alone

Part 6:
Seasons of Sorrow

Part 7:
Growing in Grace

Part 8:
Readiness to Reach Out

Acknowledgments

My gratitude runs deep for the special people who have made this book possible—

- to Jan Silvious, whom God used to teach me invaluable insights long before the book was imagined;
- to Mom, my "angel of mercy," who sent baskets of food and bushels of prayers so the writing would go uninterrupted;
- to every member of the Hope for the Heart family who work tirelessly in tandem to bring hope and healing to others, especially:
  - —June Page, who creatively prepared the project and worked closely with me, page by page,
  - —Barbara Spruill, who conscientiously managed the manuscript,
  - —Beth Stapleton, who proofed and proofed with meticulous care,
  - —Kay Deakins, my beloved secretary, who kept my schedule from sinking me.

"I thank my God . . . because of your partnership in the gospel."

Philippians 1:3,5

Introduction

Have you ever wondered, "*What should I do?*" but you had *no clue* what to do? Have you ever had friends share their problems, but you had no idea how to help solve them? Have you ever thought it was *right* "not to tell," only to learn it was *wrong* not to tell? Each of us has stood perplexed with a problem . . . totally frustrated because we couldn't "fix it." And worse, we couldn't find the first step out of the confusion! Simply put, we were stuck with our unanswered questions and unsolved problems.

Just as I finished writing this first paragraph, I was stunned to receive a phone call from "Joann." I had just been thinking, *I wish I could talk with Joann for permission to share an incident from years ago.* When I was a youth director in a large church, one of the high school girls frequently came by my downtown office to help with a variety of projects. I will never forget the day she wanted to reveal something she had never told anyone . . . but would I *promise* not to tell? I gave my word.

With much hesitation, Joann confided that for years her brother had sexually used her. In a few months he would be coming home from prison and she was scared he would continue the abuse. The fear of a painful future was written all over her face.

What could be said? I didn't know she had a brother—she had never mentioned him. I didn't know her family—they were not in church. I didn't know how to help—those days no one mentioned abuse. So I extended compassion, prayed, and kept my promise. I kept quiet. But that was the *wrong* thing to do! In my heart I wanted to help, but my ignorance rendered me helpless. To my sorrow, I was not a protector of her, nor any practical help to her.

About five years later, after I had spoken to the student body at a university in Texas, a beaming Joann came up and surprised me. To think that she was graduating from college was gratifying beyond words, especially because of the background from which she had come.

Over the years I have rarely seen or talked with Joann, yet she picked *this* time to make contact. Now a professional in the field of science, a wife and a mother, she called me from her work confessing that her life was totally out of control: her desk was a disaster, her house was in shambles, her motivation was a minus! After agreeing to try several of my simple suggestions, Joann asked if we could talk later at my home. She arrived close to 9:00 P.M. feeling a little better that at least her desk had been dealt with. But as we talked together, my heart went out to her . . . Joann didn't want to live anymore. Based on her scientific background, she knew what to ingest so that her death would look "natural." Her suicide would be a slow process—a process which she had already begun a week ago. As we talked further into the night, I heard the *error* in thinking that held her in bondage, as well as the *truth* that could set her free.

Then a thought flashed into my mind: *I've just finished writing the counseling letter on depression for this book, and it's the only letter I have here at the house. Since we are transformed by the renewing of our minds, I'll ask Joann to read the letter out loud so she can see and hear and soak in the truth.* Slowly and deliberately Joann read each sentence, periodically commenting on how each point seemed to shed light on her own problem areas. At the end of the letter, she continued to nod her head so as to say, "Yes . . . yes . . . yes, that is true." We sat in silence; God's anointing was with us. It was a holy time.

Later we talked about the impact of her victimization, and she was able to gain some insights she needed for her life. We discussed suicide and the devastating consequences it would have on her family. And we talked about follow up—specific things each of us would do. Close to midnight, as we stood by my front door I said to her, "Jesus wants to be the source of your life, your power source for change. You've tried to overcome your past, but you can't. Think of yourself as a flashlight—you are the outer casing, but you can't shine by yourself the way you were designed to shine. Just realize that when you became a Christian you received 'Christ *in* you,' the permanent presence of Almighty God (see Colossians 1:27). Like a fresh battery, Jesus is your energizer, your power source—He is the Light of the world! He is the Light to *your* world. You don't have to live in darkness anymore."

She agreed, "I've got to quit relying on myself. I need to let the Lord be the Lord of my life."

Yes! That is where she will find victory. He is the source for meeting her deepest inner needs. The Bible says: "My God will meet all your needs according to His glorious riches in Christ Jesus" (Philippians 4:19).

Today, when I reflect on those youth director years, I deeply regret that I didn't know *then* what I know *now*. But God knew what I didn't know, and He has been teaching me much "on the job." As a Bible teacher and speaker, I've been asked almost every conceivable question regarding people and their problems. Contained in this book are *real* letters from *real* people with very *real* problems. Of course, there is not just one way to answer a question, but sharing these answers is the way I've been led, with valuable input from the dedicated staff at "Hope for the Heart."

As you read this book, my request is that you read with glasses of grace. I am keenly aware that in this book of answers, a single, much more thorough book could be written on each subject with stories, illustrations, and additional practical points. But that is not the purpose of this book. Its first purpose is to open the door of understanding into life's deeper hurts to help you have a hope-filled walk toward healing. Its second purpose is to help you, "be prepared to give an answer to everyone who asks you to give the reason for the hope that you have" (1 Peter 3:15) . . . or to put it another way, to help you help others. As the "Joanns" of this world come to you crying, "Help me, I'm hurting" (and they *are* all around you), my deepest desire is that because of this book you will not be as helpless as I was years ago. May you know how to walk and talk with people through their times of hurt until their hearts are healed.

Part 1

Emotional Entrapments

1

Anger

TAMING YOUR TEMPER

Dear June,

I've always been the kind of person who is easily upset and then apologize and feel guilty. I've recently been saved and my life has changed drastically. But several weeks ago I lost my temper and became uncontrollably angry. I felt so bad about it I asked God and the person I lost my temper with to forgive me—but I still feel condemned! Why can't I have more control over my explosive anger?

Dear Exploding,

Jesus said some very encouraging words to you which are recorded in John 8:32: "Then you will know the truth, and the truth will set you free." The important truth for you to know is that when you became a Christian the Spirit of Christ was placed in you to become your defense attorney, pleading all accusations against you and securing your *total forgiveness.* (Read Romans 8:33,34.) Also

Colossians 2:13 says, "God made you alive with Christ. He forgave us all our sins." Notice the word *all.* This literally means *all the sins* you are guilty of from your past, *all the sins* you continue to commit in the present, and *all the sins* God knows you will commit in the days to come.

Although God may *convict* you of wrong behavior, He is not the author of condemning and unworthy feelings associated with guilt. *God's conviction* is a prompting in your heart to change inappropriate behavior for a more Christlike response. If you know you are forgiven and you have confessed your sin to clear your conscience and restore fellowship with God, then see God's conviction as a call for action to change. Once you completely understand that He extends the grace of *total forgiveness* toward you, then you become free to start dealing with your anger. You see, God wants you to show this same love and forgiveness to others.

It may surprise you to know that the initial emotion anger *is not a sin.* In Ephesians 4:26, God says, " 'In your anger do not sin': Do not let the sun go down while you are still angry." This actually means that anger is a God-given emotion, but it is what we *do* with our anger that determines whether it is appropriate or inappropriate. To lose your temper and explode all over others is an inappropriate response. But viewing your feelings of anger as a signal that something is wrong is appropriate.

We often use anger as a defense mechanism to protect us from emotional discomfort, therefore it is easier to stay angry than to deal honestly with the cause. Maybe it would be helpful to see your anger as the red light on the dashboard of your car. When it begins to blink it is a signal for you to go under the hood and take care of something. If you want to gain victory over your temper, when anger begins to surface, see it as a signal for you to go into your heart and look for one of these four causes.

Hurt

The heart has been wounded.

Read the Old Testament story of Joseph in Genesis 37. He was the undisputed favorite of the eleven sons of Jacob. Because the older sons allowed their hurt and jealousy to simmer into bitter anger, they eventually devised a plot to kill their own brother. When you experience rejection or emotional pain of any kind, don't allow your anger to become a blaze of bitterness.

Fear

The future is threatened.

We are all created with a God-given inner need for security. Sometimes we get angry when we *feel threatened* or *fear a change* in circumstances. A fearful heart reveals a lack of trust in God's perfect plan for your life. In 1 Samuel 18:8, Saul became angry over David's many successes on the battlefield. He felt threatened by David's popularity and feared he would lose his kingdom. His fear ignited the desire to kill David.

Frustration

Performance is not accepted.

Frustration over unmet expectations of ourselves or other people is a major source of anger. The God-given need for significance in life is erroneously fed by personal performance or by demanding that others meet and fulfill our wishes. Genesis 4:3–8 tells about two brothers who brought their offerings to God. Cain had chosen to offer what *he* wanted to give, apart from what God asked for. When his self efforts were rejected, his frustration flamed into a raging anger and he killed his brother Abel.

Injustice

A perceived right has been violated.

Everyone has an inner moral code that establishes a sense of right and wrong. When this code is violated—against yourself or others—we often become angry. As King David heard the story about a rich man who owned many sheep, slaughtering the only beloved lamb of a poor man, "David burned with anger against the man" (2 Samuel 12:5). King David was told this story because *he* had been guilty of the same injustice toward another person.

Are you beginning to understand the sources of anger? If so, are you asking, "But why does God give us the emotion of anger if it can be so damaging?" Maybe you know and understand the term *backfire*. Forest rangers who care for and protect our national parks often have to start a fire to stop an advancing fire. God works in much the same way. He uses the emotion of anger to turn you back toward a larger blaze that is consuming your spiritual growth. He allows fiery trials so that you can learn to tame your temper and grow in the likeness of Christ. "In this you greatly rejoice, though now for a little while you may have to suffer grief in all kinds of trials. These have come so that your faith . . . may be proved genuine . . ." (1 Peter 1:6,7).

Taming the Temper

Acknowledge your anger is out of control. "He who conceals his sins does not prosper, but whoever confesses and renounces them finds mercy" (Proverbs 28:13).

Apologize to anyone you have hurt or offended. "Therefore, if you are offering your gift at the altar and there remember that your brother has something against you, leave your gift there in front of the altar. First go and be reconciled to your brother; then come and offer your gift" (Matthew 5:23,24).

Ask God to help you identify the cause. "Search me, O God, and know my heart; test me and know my anxious thoughts. See if there is any offensive way in me, and lead me in the way everlasting" (Psalm 139:23,24).

Abandon your demands. "It is better to take refuge in the LORD than to trust in man" (Psalm 118:8).

- When you feel *hurt* or *rejected,* choose to rest in God's undying love for you. "The LORD appeared to us in the past, saying: 'I have loved you with an everlasting love; I have drawn you with loving-kindness. I will build you up again and you will be rebuilt, O Virgin

Israel. Again you will take up your tambourines and go out to dance with the joyful' " (Jeremiah 31:3,4).

- When you are *fearful* or *feel threatened,* choose to look to God for your security. "I sought the LORD, and he answered me; he delivered me from all my fears" (Psalm 34:4).
- When you are *frustrated* or *disappointed* in others, choose to turn loose of your expectations and place your hope in God only. "Find rest, O my soul, in God alone; my hope comes from him. He alone is my rock and my salvation; he is my fortress, I will not be shaken. My salvation and my honor depend on God; he is my mighty rock, my refuge. Trust in him at all times, O people; pour out your hearts to him, for God is our refuge" (Psalm 62:5–8).
- When your personal sense of what should be just and fair is violated, choose to acknowledge that God is sovereign over all circumstances. "If it is possible, as far as it depends on you, live at peace with everyone. Do not take revenge, my friends, but leave room for God's wrath, for it is written: 'It is mine to avenge; I will repay,' says the Lord" (Romans 12:18,19).

Apply forgiveness to others. "Therefore, as God's chosen people, holy and dearly loved, clothe yourselves with compassion, kindness, humility, gentleness and patience. Bear with each other and forgive whatever grievances you may have against one another. Forgive as the Lord forgave you. And over all these virtues put on love, which binds them all together in perfect unity" (Colossians 3:12–14).

Articulate your feelings gently. "A gentle answer turns away wrath, but a harsh word stirs up anger" (Proverbs 15:1).

Aim for peace and holiness. "Make every effort to live in peace with all men and to be holy; without holiness no one will see the Lord. See to it that no one misses the grace of God and that no bitter root grows up to cause trouble and defile many" (Hebrews 12:14,15).

As you begin your journey to gain control over your temper, there is another important truth for you to know. When you became a Christian and received total forgiveness from God through Christ, you also *received access to the resources of Christ* to respond to others in a godly way. "I can do everything through him who gives me strength" (Philippians 4:13). You can be free from living for the acceptance of others. You have the power to no longer become angered when people don't meet your expectations. And finally, you never have to become out of control because *Christ is in control!*

2

Depression

Stormy Weather

Dear June,

Recently I've suffered the losses of a dear relationship, my employment, my sobriety, and my sense of self-worth. Instead of turning to the Lord I spend most of my time just wondering why I am even here. I find that I cannot even pray; it seems useless and not real to me. Frankly, I don't know if God even exists and if He does, I hate Him for what He has allowed to happen. Where is my faith? Full of anger and self-pity, I often drink and am continually depressed. Is there any hope for me?

Dear Deeply Depressed,

Your letter reveals how much you are hurting and how dark and cold are your days. The storm clouds of despair seem to have unleashed their tears on your soul and you see no release in sight. Although you may not feel there is hope for your heart, the Lord assures you there is. In Jeremiah

29:11 He lets you know how significant you are to Him saying, *"I know the plans I have for you . . . plans to prosper you and not to harm you, plans to give you hope and a future."*

There is hope. God's hope for you is not wishful thinking—it is absolute assurance! *Assurance* that your life has meaning and purpose . . . and that you are *precious* to Him. Yes, precious. Isaiah 43:3,4 says, "I am the LORD, your God . . . you are precious and honored in my sight, and . . . I love you. . . ." God dearly loves you—He loves you *personally.* He wants to part the dark clouds of depression and enfold you in the light of His love.

Clouds of Depression

What Is Depression?

Depression is an umbrella word which covers prolonged feelings ranging from mild discouragement to intense despair. Psychologically, it is a state in which the heart feels pressed down (de-pressed) and unable to experience joy. Although most people think of depression only in the emotional arena, the black clouds of depression bring darkness upon the whole person: spirit, soul, and body.

What Causes Depression?

Depression is caused by different problems in different areas of people's lives. Each person is comprised of three parts as seen in 1 Thessalonians 5:23: "May your whole *spirit, soul* and *body* be kept blameless. . . ." Since all of these areas are interconnected, a problem that starts in one area can contribute to problems in the other areas. Therefore, you will again be warmed by the sun's glow as you learn how to deal with depression in all three of of these areas.

Confronting the Clouds— The Body

First, See a Physician

To dissipate the dark clouds of depression a vital first step is consulting a doctor who will take your depression seriously and who will give you a thorough medical evaluation. Various physical problems can contribute to depression. For example, in manic-depression (characterized by extreme highs and lows) one of the major factors is a biochemical imbalance which is usually treated successfully with medication. Unfortunately, many Christians fear being labeled unspiritual if they seek help for their depression, yet by doing nothing they can suffer needlessly. Sometimes medication is even needed for a period of time to "level out" mountainous swings so that those in the throes of depression can see truth and walk on level ground. In Ezekiel 47:12 God made "leaves for healing." Therefore, medicine is biblical. However, medicine should be used, not to numb the pain or to escape it, but to help a person process the pain. Additionally, medication should be the last avenue—tried only after all other steps have been taken.

Fight Depression Physically

Most people who are depressed experience loss of energy and initiative. It may even seem like too much trouble to get out of bed in the morning. However, physically you can help your body fight depression.

- *Maintain a regular schedule of activity.* Be involved in church activities; accept invitations to be with others—even if you don't feel like it.

- *Exercise each day.* Although you may feel fatigued, a brisk thirty-minute walk may increase certain chemicals in your brain which help relieve depression.

- *Play Christian praise music.* The inspirational words and melodies of praise music provide an emotional uplift in contrast to the more depressing lyrics of most country and rock music.

- *Spend time in the sun.* Research indicates that lack of exposure to sunlight can trigger or worsen depression.

- *Eat a balanced diet.* To keep your energy level up, eat regular meals at regular times—even if you are not hungry. Be aware that alcohol is a depressant and too much sugar gives you a blood-sugar high that eventually drops you into the "sugar blues."

- *Regulate your sleep.* If you have trouble sleeping, don't take naps during the day. Avoid caffeine after 4 P.M., exercise each day, take a warm bath, and drink warm milk before bedtime. If you are sleeping too much, set your alarm. Get up at a regular time each day, plan your daily activities, and stick to that plan. Routine activity will help your body readjust and fight depression.

Clearing the Clouds—
The Soul

The soul, sometimes called the personality, is your *mind, will,* and *emotions.* Typically, depression descends upon the soul after a severe loss—the heart is "pressed down" like a small foam pillow under a heavy iron. When you have lost a significant relationship whether by rejection, divorce, or death, it is normal for your heart to be "depressed." However, after a period of time normal healing should have occurred. If the heart has not "resumed its natural shape," that heart could be in a state of depression.

No matter how long the sky has been overcast or how long your soul has been downcast, you can be confident that your heart can respond again and say with the psalmist, "I am still confident of this: I will see the goodness of the LORD in the land of the living" (Psalm 27:13).

Your Emotions—Face Your Feelings

Often people who are depressed have difficulty expressing their feelings in a healthy way. A common cause of depression is buried feelings due to loss; ignored or denied feelings won't go away. They are buried alive, deep inside your soul, where they fester and create an infection that produces poison in your body. That is why it is vital to face your feelings.

Bring your heartache and hurts, your anxiety and anger, your fear and frustration to Jesus. Pour out your heart to Him and receive His comfort. He alone understands the depth of your pain. Hebrews 4:15,16 assures us, "We do not have a high priest who is unable to sympathize with our weaknesses, but we have one who has been tempted in every way, just as we are—yet was without sin. Let us then approach the throne of grace with confidence, so that we may receive mercy and find grace to help us in our time of need."

*Your **Mind**—Line Up Your Thinking*

What you think can be the key to overcoming chronic depression. You need to fill up your thinking with the Lord's thinking—fill your mind with God's perspective and promises. Since Romans 12:2 says you are "transformed by the renewing of your mind" write several passages on index cards and read them several times a day.

By looking at God's Word you can discover God's purpose for *allowing* the painful losses in your life. Since God is the Redeemer, He has a purpose for allowing everything; the storms in your life are no accident. Don't miss seeing God's design for allowing your depression. From Scripture, discern how depression can:

- *Warn you that something is wrong.* "Before I was afflicted I went astray, but now I obey your word" (Psalm 119:67).
- *Reveal your weakness.* The Lord said, "My grace is sufficient for you, for my power is made perfect in weakness" (2 Corinthians 12:9).
- *Cause you to rely on Him.* "So do not fear, for I am with you; do not be dismayed, for I am your God.

I will strengthen you and help you; I will uphold you with my righteous right hand" (Isaiah 41:10).

- *Refine your character.* "See, I have refined you, though not as silver; I have tested you in the furnace of affliction" (Isaiah 48:10).
- *Develop your perseverance and maturity.* "Consider it pure joy, my brothers, whenever you face trials of many kinds, because you know that the testing of your faith develops perseverance. Perseverance must finish its work so that you may be mature and complete, not lacking anything" (James 1:2–4).
- *Increase your compassion for others.* "[He] comforts us in all our troubles, so that we can comfort those in any trouble with the comfort we ourselves have received from God" (2 Corinthians 1:4).

Your Will—Choose to Rely on Your Redeemer

People who have prolonged depression usually feel that life has stripped them of their choices. They feel stranded in the middle of the storm with no real options. But that is far from the truth. While it is true that life is sprinkled with unavoidable discouragement, you *can avoid* letting your mind become drenched with discouragement. That is your choice; it's an act of *the will.*

After an initial cloudburst, you can choose to *rely on yourself* for relief or get underneath God's umbrella of protection and *rely on Him.* Jesus said, "Do not let your hearts be troubled. Trust in God; trust also in me" (John 14:1). You can choose to trust the Lord with your life; *He is worthy of your trust.* As an act of your will you can choose to pray a prayer of yieldedness:

> *Dear Lord, I feel drenched with heavy discouragement. The weight is too heavy for me. I need You to be my strength because my strength is not enough. I'm relying on You to redeem me from my messes. Lord Jesus, be my Lord. I yield my mind to Your mind and my will to Your will. In Your precious name I pray, Amen.*

Conquering the Clouds—
The Spirit

God Met Elijah's Need

Your *human spirit* is the origin of your deepest inner needs for *love, significance,* and *security.* Your human spirit is designed by God to "house" the Holy Spirit. If one of these needs is not met or seriously threatened, depression can set in as seen in the prophet Elijah's life. Although he had been greatly used by God before the prophets of Baal, when his life was threatened, he ran for his life and spiraled down into a suicidal depression crying, "I have had enough, LORD. . . . Take my life" (1 Kings 19:4). Frightened and frantic, Elijah did not feel loved, significant, or secure. But God did not get mad at him—instead He met him at his point of need.

Elijah was depressed in body, soul, and spirit. So, God first gave him food and rest. Then God dealt with his soul (his mind, will, and emotions) by gently telling him *truth* that he needed to *act* upon. In the end the Lord knew it would change his *emotions.* Ultimately God met Elijah's spiritual need by proving Himself trustworthy to the prophet even though Elijah, for a time, had lost trust because of how he was seeing his circumstances. In the same way that God ministered to Elijah, He wants to minister to you.

God Will Meet Your Need

It's easy to get focused on your present problems and to see the whole world through a gloomy black filter rather than from God's bright and broad perspective. If you only see your struggles, it will seem as though the stormy weather will never end. But if you fix your eyes on the Lord, who is *over your troubles,* you will see how He sees you: *dearly loved, significant,* and *secure* in His arms of love. Isaiah 40:11 says, "He tends his flock like a shepherd: he gathers the lambs in his arms and carries them close to his heart; he gently leads those that have young."

You may not have strength to hold onto Him, but He will hold onto you. He is your refuge and safety. You are so important to the Lord that even if you were the only person on earth, Jesus would still have given His life for you. As a child of God, you have immeasurable worth and value. No matter how dark and depressing your clouds, God's sun always shines above them and *He* will eventually break through to you.

> *Why are you downcast, O my soul? Why so disturbed within me? Put your hope in God, for I will yet praise him, my Savior and my God* (Psalm 42:11).

3

Guilt

True or False?

Dear June,

I have been a Christian for a few years now and have been trying to be faithful and live a holy life for God. But recently I made a terrible mistake. I gave in to temptation and did something that I know is wrong in God's sight. The guilt of my sin is tearing me apart inside. I have repeatedly asked God to forgive me, but I am so ashamed. My guilt and shame won't go away. Please help me in my walk with the Lord. I feel like such a sinner. Can God ever use me again?

Dear Guilt-Ridden,

The answer to your question is undeniably *yes!* The Lord can and will use you again as you learn to live in dependence on Him. You obviously have a repentant heart. Yet, since your "terrible mistake" was committed *after* becoming a Christian, you seem unable to feel God's full forgiveness. Consequently, I think you will find these questions helpful:

- When Jesus died on the cross, how many of your sins were in the future?
- Before you were born, how many of your sins did God know about?
- How many sins did Christ know you would commit after becoming a Christian?
- For how many of your sins did Jesus die?

All, all, all, *yes all!* Jesus paid the penalty for *all* your sin—past, present, and future. As Hebrews 10:10 says, "We have been made holy through the sacrifice of the body of Jesus Christ once for *all.*"

I have yet to meet a person who has not sinned after becoming a Christian. Yet the guilt over your sin is further confirmation of your deepest need to be dependent on Christ, who indwells you. Realize that, as a Christian, you literally have "Christ in you" to be your source of strength and your resource for life (see Colossians 1:27). Since He is your source to keep you from sin, personalize the promise in Philippians 4:13, "I can do everything through him who gives me strength."

God takes no delight in a Christian groveling in guilt. So how can you find the freedom from guilt you so long for? You have already taken the first steps: agreeing with God that what you did was wrong (confession), and turning from your sin (brokenness or repentance). Now you need to learn to distinguish true guilt from false guilt by focusing not on your feelings, but on the facts.

How to Distinguish False Guilt from True Guilt

True Guilt—Based on Fact

True guilt is based on your recognition of the fact that you have sinned. Note David's honesty in Psalm 32:5: "I acknowledged my sin to you and did not cover up my iniquity . . . and you forgave the guilt of my sin." How did God respond? With forgiveness. God's response is the same for you. First John 1:9 says, "If we confess our sins, he is faithful and just and will forgive us our sins and purify us from all unrighteousness." God is faithful—He will always do what He says He will do. Not only has God forgiven you, He has also *removed the sin* from you. (See Psalm 103:8–12.)

Write out and memorize these helpful verses:

Psalm 32:5	Romans 8:1
Psalm 103:12	2 Corinthians 7:10
Proverbs 28:13	1 John 1:9

As a conscientious Father, God sometimes allows you to experience the consequences of your sin to encourage you not to sin. (Read Hebrews 12:4–11.) Often these consequences bring pain or loss to others. If you have wronged a person, you need to right it. If you have stolen something, you need to return it. If you have lied to someone, you need to confess it. Ask the Spirit of Christ what to do, and then rely on His strength to do it.

One role of the Holy Spirit is counselor—He is your conscience and "convictor" so that you can live with a clear conscience (see John 16:8). In humility, ask for His help:

- Pray for God's Spirit to reveal your *true* offense (see Psalm 139:23,24).
- Pray for the courage to ask forgiveness and, if necessary, make restitution (see Matthew 5:23,24).
- Pray for God to provide the proper timing and circumstance (see Psalm 32:8).
- Pray for Him to prepare the hearts of those you have offended (see Proverbs 16:7).
- Pray for the ability to accept God's forgiveness—even if others are unforgiving (see Psalm 103:10–12).

False Guilt—Based on Feelings

Ironically, confession does not resolve false guilt. False guilt arises when you blame yourself even though you've committed no wrong or *when you continue to blame yourself after you've confessed and turned from your sin.* Revelation 12:10 says Satan is the "accuser of our brothers." He loves to burden believers with false guilt and condemnation. Some of his favorite strategies are: bringing up the past, reminding you of your failures, and making you feel unforgiven and unaccepted by God.

In contrast, the Holy Spirit never condemns true Christians—Romans 8:1 says, "There is now no condemnation for those who are in Christ Jesus." Yes, He grieves over unconfessed sin, but He also produces within you a desire to change and grow. "For it is God who works in you to will [have the desire to do His will] and to act according to his good purpose" (Philippians 2:13).

The next time the viewing screen of your mind begins to replay your repented sins, realize that this taunting is from Satan the accuser to discourage you. Ask yourself: "What am I hearing?" (accusation) "What am I feeling?" (guilt) "What are the facts?" (fully forgiven). Use Scripture as your standard to determine true and false guilt. Since you have received Jesus Christ as your personal Savior, and since the Savior died to take away your sin, choose to focus on God's truth. Turn Romans 8:1 into a prayer: "Thank You, Father, that You don't condemn me and don't want me to condemn myself. These feelings of false guilt are not valid because I've accepted Christ's sacrifice and turned from my sin."

How to Gain Victory Over Guilt

Confession

Conviction of *unconfessed* sin is a sign that something should be confessed. God uses "good guilt" to soften hardened hearts and to prompt genuine confession. "He who conceals his sin does not prosper, but whoever confesses and renounces them finds mercy" (Proverbs 28:13).

Say "Lord, You see everything. I admit that I . . ."

Brokenness

Spiritual brokenness does not destroy value—it increases value. A wild horse whose will is not broken is not really valuable. The "broken" horse becomes more and more valuable as he becomes trained and easily turns with the slightest tug of the rider's reins. God shows His delight in a heart broken over sin and a will broken and yielded before the Savior. "The sacrifices of God are a broken spirit; a broken and contrite heart; O God, you will not despise" (Psalm 51:17).

Make this commitment: "Lord, in deep sorrow I see my sin and I will turn from my sin."

Forgiveness

Why bear the burden for your sin when Christ has already borne it for you? Jesus took your punishment so that you would not have to bear the weight of permanent separation from God. Your brokenness releases the weight of feeling emotional separation from God. Are you willing to take God at His Word? Choose to accept His forgiveness and forgive yourself. *In order to feel forgiven, accept Christ's sacrifice and forgiveness as a gift of grace*—unmerited and undeserved. Take comfort in 1 Peter 3:18, "Christ died for sins once for all, the righteous for the unrighteous, to bring you to God."

When that "terrible mistake" flashes across your mind, immediately turn it into a prayer: "Thank You, Father, for Your forgiveness—I accept as a gift Your mercy and Your grace."

Dependence

You said you've been trying to live a holy life for God. Do you know that God never intended for you to live the Christian life in your own strength? In fact, He knew you couldn't. Paul understood this when, in Galatians 2:20, he wrote, "I have been crucified with Christ and I no longer live, but Christ lives in me. The life I live in the body, I live by faith in the Son of God, who loved me and gave himself for me." The strength to live a godly life comes from Christ living in you. Your responsibility is to submit yourself to

Jesus, allowing Him to transform you and live out His character through you.

Let me assure you, your sin did not catch God by surprise! Your Provider even had a plan for it: He provided *good guilt* so that you would turn from your sin in brokenness and live in dependence on Him. Then He provided Christ *in* you to live a *guilt-free* life. So, let go of past guilt—it has already served its purpose. Why continue to review it when God can't even remember it!

> *For I will forgive their wickedness, and will remember their sins no more* (Jeremiah 31:34).

4

Stress

Beating Burnout

Dear June,

I am currently the Director of Children's Education at my church. I'm married, have two children, and work part-time in addition to teaching piano. With church activities, phone calls, thank-you notes, training, teaching, homemaking, being homework helper, mother, and wife, how can I have time to disciple, reach out to the unsaved, and discover again the true basics of being a Christian? I am so tired at the beginning and end of the day that I can't function. Am I burning both ends of the wick? I think so!

Dear Burning Out,

You are not alone—stress has snuffed the light of life out of many people whose hearts were right but priorities were wrong. Let me assure you, as you prioritize your most essential responsibilities, you can keep from burning out.

How can you keep your candle burning strong without all the stress? You've already taken the first step—seeing the need for change. Since you indicate you want to do what God wants, consider what activities are consuming your time.

What Takes Your Time?

Some people think that burning out because of busyness is so noble that they deserve the Medal of Honor. However, don't adopt this mind-set, for the Lord thinks the opposite. ✓ He wants His light of love to *shine out* to the world through you—not *burn out!* Getting back to the basics *will happen* as you spend time alone with the Lord, asking Him to reorder your priorities.

How do you check your priorities? Start with this helpful assignment:

- Over the next week make a detailed list of everything to which you give your time—everything!
- Evaluate each activity, deciding whether your involvement is Spirit-led, people-pressured, or self-motivated.
- Add any priorities you think *should* have been included (such as special family times, regular exercise, adequate sleep, healthy eating, one day of rest each week).
- Number each priority in terms of importance.
- Eliminate those activities which are not Spirit-led—remember, the *good* in life is the enemy of the *best* in life.

- Ask an organized person in your life to help you. Since the most difficult step in getting started is the first step, many organized people would enjoy the challenge of helping someone who is willing to be helped. Pray for the Lord to provide you with an "accountability partner": "Two are better than one, because they have a good return for their work" (Ecclesiastes 4:9).

Major on the Majors

Many people are on a beeline for burnout because they are too busy majoring on the minors. Keep in mind: If you try to juggle too many balls, you will eventually drop them all!

What should your priorities be? Jesus pinpointed what is most important: "'Love the Lord your God with all your heart and with all your soul and with all your mind.' This is the first and greatest commandment. And the second is like it: 'Love your neighbor as yourself' " (Matthew 22:37–39). Since the word "neighbor" literally means "one living or located near another," realize that the family members in your home are your nearest neighbors. Therefore, your relationship with the Lord is your first priority—a love relationship so intimate that you can know His heart and, thus, His will. And your second priority is your own family. Your extended neighbors, career, church work, and other interests come *after* the Lord and your family.

As you learn to major on the majors, consider 1 Timothy 5:8, "If anyone does not provide for his relatives, and especially for his immediate family, he has denied the faith and is worse than an unbeliever."

While there are hundreds of good deeds you could do outside your home, one of your highest priorities must be your family. For example, if you fail to be a "helper" to your husband because you are too busy helping others, he will be hurt, your heart will be heavy, and you will not have harmony in your home—and that equals *stress!* (The same is true if he doesn't make you a priority.)

In terms of reaching out to others, right now your prime discipleship opportunity is your children—devote quality time to building their Christian character. Spend regular, quality, one-on-one time with each child . . . perhaps over a double-dip ice-cream cone! Introduce conversation about values, ask their opinions, and *listen, listen, listen.* Verbally praise everything they do right.

What about reaching out to the unsaved? Certainly, you can reach out to others as you let the Lord orchestrate opportunities *naturally* . . . as you live the Christian life before your neighbors, as you show interest in other parents at your children's sporting events. God knows the willingness of your heart to be available to Him, and He will honor your care and concern.

Is it possible you are burning out because you are burdened with tasks that the Lord never initiated? As you look at Ecclesiastes 4:6, you can see there is a better way: "Better one handful with tranquillity than two handfuls with toil and chasing after the wind." Let these points help you prioritize what is most important:

- Look at what God has initiated and called you to do.
- Drop out of involvements that He has not initiated.

- Pray to follow only *the Lord's* agenda.
- Make a daily "to do" list.
- Number each task, beginning with the most important to the least.
- Try to tackle one task—to completion—at a time.

Use Timesaving Tips

In your letter you mentioned many tasks difficult to find time to do. Here are a few simple suggestions that will enable you to accomplish these in the quickest way. Bunch your thank-you notes together and begin answering them without allowing yourself to get diverted to any other task. You will find yourself "on a roll" and they will all be written much faster. Likewise, answer all phone calls in one block period of time. You will streamline your own talking because of all the other calls yet to be placed.

When a homemaking priority seems too big, just remember, "How do you eat an elephant? One bite at a time!" For example, if your priority was to clean out every drawer and closet in your home, you would have to break that project down into bite-size chunks. Beginning in the living room, take one room at a time, going through one piece of furniture at a time. For the items that need moved, have three boxes ready—1) trash, 2) give away, and 3) place elsewhere. Don't forget, God is a God of order and because you have "Christ in you" (Colossians 1:27), you have His very presence indwelling you. The primary point is that whatever God prioritizes for you, His empowering presence will do *through* you. First Thessalonians 5:24 says, "The one who calls you is faithful and *He will do it*" (emphasis added).

Discipline Yourself with Don'ts

For most people, it's easier to say yes than no when others request time. However, often you need to say no to others so that you can say yes to God. In 1 Corinthians 6:12 Paul says, " 'Everything is permissible for me'—but not everything is beneficial." If you apply these "Don'ts for Decision Making," you will beat burnout:

- Don't focus on doing *more* tasks, but on doing *fewer* tasks well.
- Don't accept impossible deadlines—factor in extra "pad" time.
- Don't leave decisions hanging—decide immediately on a course of action each time you can.
- Don't let the desires of others dictate how you spend your time.
- Don't assume that the "emergencies" of others are your emergencies.
- Don't say *yes* when you should say *no*.

If you have difficulty saying no, evaluate who has your highest loyalty. Take a heart inventory with Galatians 1:10, "Am I now trying to win the approval of men, or of God? Or am I trying to please men? If I were still trying to please men, I would not be a servant of Christ."

When God does not give you a green light and you need to turn down involvement in an activity, you can say, "I'm so honored that you would ask me to ________. However, because of other time commitments I regret that I must say no." If you are being pressured to change your mind, repeat your regret. Staying Spirit-led will alleviate your stress.

Come Closer to Christ

Are you aware that your pressing circumstances can either *stress* your life or *bless* your life? Your burdens can either come between you and the Lord or draw you closer to Him? That is why Jesus said, "Take my yoke upon you and learn from me, for I am gentle and humble in heart, and you will find rest for your souls. For my yoke is easy and my burden is light" (Matthew 11:29,30). Consider the story of Mary and Martha. Martha was busy *doing* everything she could think of for Jesus. However, she was harried, hassled and headed for burnout. Meanwhile, Mary was sitting at His feet "listening to what He said." Then Jesus said, "Martha, Martha . . . you are worried and upset about many things, but only one thing is needed. Mary has chosen what is better, and it will not be taken away from her." Martha was frazzled doing things *for* her Master, whereas Mary was focused on time *with* her Master. (Read Luke 10:38–42.)

The Christian life is not a pile of projects or principles, but a *Person—Christ Himself*. Pray that you will come closer to Christ—

- Take time in the Bible each day to "be still, and know that I am God" (Psalm 46:10).

- Meditate on how Jesus did not succumb to stress. "When they hurled their insults at him, he did not retaliate; when he suffered, he made no threats. Instead he entrusted himself to him who judges justly" (1 Peter 2:23).
- Talk openly with the Lord about your fears and frazzled feelings. Look to the Lord alone to be your Burden-Bearer. "Come to me, all you who are weary and burdened, and I will give you rest" (Matthew 11:28).
- Exchange your frail strength for the full strength of Christ. "I can do everything through him who gives me strength" (Philippians 4:13).
- Allow the Lord to be your Need-Meeter. "And my God will meet all your needs according to his glorious riches in Christ Jesus" (Philippians 4:19).
- Pray that your Provider will reveal your real priorities. "But seek first his kingdom and his righteousness, and all these things will be given to you as well" (Matthew 6:33).

My friend, guarding your time with God can be difficult because of outside pressure, but realize this truth: *The Lord allows pressure in life to press you closer to Him.* Since Jesus is "the light of the world" (John 8:12), the closer you are to Him, the more light you will have in life. And the more light you have in life, the less you will have stress! As you let the Lord express His life through you, you will naturally "let your light shine before men" (Matthew 5:16). And that's the best way not to burn out!

5

Temptation

Snared by an Affair

Dear June,

I am in an adulterous relationship with a married man whom I love very much, but I want out because I know it is wrong, wrong, wrong. I've tried to break away twice but he totally ignored my request. Why are we so weak? Why can't he be faithful to his wife? I cry to God and it seems I get strength, but when I see him again or when night falls, I wind up with him again. Please help me!

Dear Snared,

Thank you for being so open and honest in sharing the defeat you're experiencing in temptation. I can sense the tremendous tension, conflict, and discouragement you are feeling as you battle the pull between your godly conscience and your fleshly desires. You say you know your relationship is "wrong, wrong, wrong," and yet you have been unable to break off your involvement.

The Way Around Temptation

To be tempted or have tempting thoughts is not wrong, but *acting* on tempting desires becomes sin. Everyone is tempted . . . even Jesus experienced temptation (see Hebrews 4:15). But taking part in an adulterous relationship is a *choice you are making*. You cannot stand before God and say, "*He* ignores my requests to break it off" or "Why can't *he* be faithful to his wife?" No one is accountable for your actions but *yourself*. We all tend to blame someone else, our circumstances or even God, but this is just avoiding *responsibility*. The Lord makes this clear in James 1:13–15: "When tempted, no one should say, 'God is tempting me.' For God cannot be tempted by evil, nor does he tempt anyone; but each one is tempted when, by his own evil desire, he is dragged away and enticed. Then, after desire has conceived, it gives birth to sin; and sin, when it is full-grown, gives birth to death."

The Way into Temptation

Let me encourage you to come to the Lord with the same openness and honesty you expressed in your letter. The description of your situation and the feelings you have closely parallel the situation and feelings Paul expressed in Romans 7:19: "What I do is not the good I want to do; no, the evil I do not want to do—this I keep on doing." Now notice the hope that is offered in the next chapter of Romans. It says, you have a *choice* and you have *Christ*. You can *choose* not to be controlled by your sinful desires because, if you are born again, you have the Spirit of Christ living in you—enabling you to resist any temptation you want to resist! "You, however, are controlled not by the sinful nature but by the Spirit, if the Spirit of God lives in you" (Romans 8:9).

Many times we *know* what we *want* to do, but our hearts seem to go a different direction. For example: Imagine yourself driving much faster than the speed limit allows because you are late for a theater performance. You really don't *want* to break the law because you *know* to do so would be wrong, but your heart pushes you to go faster so you will not miss the first scene. Now what would help you act on what you *know* is right, instead of acting out your desire not to be late? When you see a policeman sitting in his car at the next corner, you are reminded of the consequences of speeding and your foot immediately applies the brakes. This is because your greatest desire now is to avoid the consequences of your unlawful behavior. This same principle applies whenever we do that which we know we should not do. We follow our *feelings* instead of *fearing the consequences* of sin. This is exactly why Proverbs 1:7 tells us, "The fear of the LORD is the beginning of knowledge, but fools despise wisdom and discipline."

To help get your feelings moving in the direction you *know* they should travel, memorize the following Scriptures. Say them over and over again until they pave every road that leads to your heart.

- Proverbs 5:21–23
- Proverbs 6:27,28
- Proverbs 6:32
- Romans 8:13
- 1 Corinthians 6:18
- 2 Corinthians 5:10
- Galatians 6:7
- Hebrews 13:4

Once you really understand that you are trying to get your need for love and acceptance met through an illicit relationship, your choice may become even more clear. We have all been given this inner need for unconditional love, and since it is given by God, it can be met only in God's way. It appears you may be acting out of a wrong belief system. Are you thinking, "My need for love and affection is so strong I cannot resist responding to that which momentarily seems to satisfy these desires"? If that is the case, then *what you are telling yourself is a lie!* The truth is, "God designed me with inner needs which *He* will meet, either by bringing His choice into my life, or by meeting those needs *Himself.*" It is *impossible* for your needs to be met through a counterfeit relationship! "And my God will meet all your needs according to his glorious riches in Christ Jesus" (Philippians 4:19).

The Way Out of Temptation

Not only does God promise to meet all your needs, He also *provides the way of escape.* "No temptation has seized you except what is common to man. And God is faithful; he will not let you be tempted beyond what you can bear. But when you are tempted, he will also provide a way out so that you can stand up under it" (1 Corinthians 10:13). But remember, the way of escape is not in *your* own power or ability to say no, but rather *in the ability of God's Holy Spirit within you* (Christ) to say no. (Read Titus 2:11–14.)

These practical steps will help you appropriate the strength that is yours in Christ. This strength is the desire and ability to overcome temptation.

The Way of Escape

***E**xpose your sin to God*

Confess your sin to God and admit you are making choices that are disobedient and grievous to God.

> Nothing in all creation is hidden from God's sight. Everything is uncovered and laid bare before the eyes of him to whom we must give account (Hebrews 4:13).

***S**ee the consequences of untamed temptation*

Realize you are not a victim of your desires. You are choosing to continue an adulterous relationship for which God will hold you responsible.

> Do not be deceived: God cannot be mocked. A man reaps what he sows. The one who sows to please his sinful nature, from that nature will reap destruction; the one who sows to please the Spirit, from the Spirit will reap eternal life (Galatians 6:7,8).

***C**hoose to trust in God*

Understand the needs you are trying to get met, and believe God will meet those needs Himself, in His own timing.

> Those who know your name will trust in you, for you, LORD, have never forsaken those who seek you (Psalm 9:10).

Act on God's provision

Remind yourself that your old sin nature died with Jesus on the cross and you now have Christ Himself living within you to govern your behavior.

> In the same way, count yourselves dead to sin but alive to God in Christ Jesus (Romans 6:11).

Protect yourself from new temptation

- Refuse to see this man again.
- Stop calling or receiving calls from him.
- Make yourself accountable to someone.
- Pursue healthy relationships with committed Christians.

> Flee from all this, and pursue righteousness, godliness, faith, love, endurance and gentleness (1 Timothy 6:11).

√ *Experience the deliverance of Christ*

Escaping emotional and physical entanglement is never easy, but as you submit your will to Christ when you are faced with temptation, He will set you free. In this way you will bring honor to our holy God.

> Call upon me in the day of trouble; I will deliver you, and you will honor me (Psalm 50:15).

I pray that you will choose *today* to be obedient to God and break away from this adulterous relationship. God is patiently waiting to give you the *grace to escape.*

> *My grace is sufficient for you, for my power is made perfect in weakness* (2 Corinthians 12:9).

PART
2

Acting Out Addictions

6

Alcoholism

Caring Enough to Confront

Dear June,

My husband is an alcoholic. He knows it, he needs help, he refuses to get it, and says he's got to make up his own mind. I agree! I pray several times a day and I have a lot of other people praying. I don't know if I should just give up or what. It seems like the harder I pray, the worse he drinks. Am I the cause of all this by praying? I don't know where to turn for help.

Dear Perplexed Pray-er,

Let me assure you: *Neither you nor your prayers are responsible for your husband's drinking*. No matter what his circumstances are, *he* has chosen to drink. The normal path for an alcoholic is to become increasingly needy of alcohol.

God wants you to pray and tells you to pray, but He also expects you to *act in faith* on your prayers. This simply means, if you are praying yet not holding your husband accountable for his inappropriate actions, you are *pleading for God's help* while at the same time *hindering His help*. You have become an enabler—helping him continue in his destructive pattern of drinking by making excuses for him and protecting him from negative consequences.

Don't be discouraged . . . God knows your heart. These practical steps will express your love and faith as you create caring boundaries, confront the crisis, and choose to be content.

Create Caring Boundaries

> Each of you should look not only to your own interests, but also to the interests of others (Philippians 2:4).

Give up expectations of change. (See Psalm 62:5.)

> Your expectations can feel like demands to your mate, and you need to let them go. Realize that as much as he may dislike his destructive drinking, he can't change on his own—if he could have, he would have! Set a mental boundary for yourself: Put your hope not in your husband, but in your relationship with the Lord.

Detach from the problem. (See Psalm 25:15.)

> Don't become addicted to your husband's addiction cycle. Don't let his problem be the central focus of your life. His problem is *his* problem. Since he may never change, say to yourself, "I am not responsible

for his problem, but I am responsible for my responses and my relationship with the Lord."

Shift your focus to your responses. (See Proverbs 19:22a.)

Instead of focusing on his wrong behavior, concentrate on your right response. Let your highest aim be *agape love*—a love which is a commitment to seek his highest good no matter what he does or doesn't do. When tempted to be bitter or give him the silent treatment, continue to ask, "What is most loving for him? Lord, express Your love through me."

Set loving boundaries. (See Proverbs 14:12.)

Carefully consider how you may have enabled your husband to continue drinking without facing consequences. Are you making excuses and protecting him? Write your patterns down. Lovingly tell your husband that you will no longer hide or support his drinking because to do so is not seeking his highest good and is not in his best interest. Say, "I see that my past help has actually hurt you—it prolonged getting the help you really want and need."

Communicate your pain. (See Proverbs 16:21.)

Gently but honestly tell your husband how his behavior is affecting you and others. You might say, "It's very painful for me that your drinking has come between us. I feel hurt that we don't seem as close as we once were. I want you to know how much I miss you." Use "I" statements ("I feel hurt") as opposed to "you" statements ("You're so insensitive") which will put him on the defensive.

Confront the Crisis

Each of you must put off falsehood and speak truthfully to his neighbor (Ephesians 4:25).

Pray for wisdom and direction in helping your husband. (See Proverbs 2:6.)

Avoid negative, judgmental attitudes toward your husband. (See Romans 14:13.)

Choose a Christian leader trained in crisis intervention. (See Proverbs 19:20.)

Gather caring family and friends to confront your husband. (See Proverbs 15:22.)

In meeting #1 (without *your husband):* Pray together and discuss specific, recent examples of your husband's hurtful behavior—examples which need to be shared with him. Plan what each person will say and in what order each one will speak.

It would be helpful to have a Christian mediator trained in crisis intervention to meet with you. Also consider asking your husband's employer and your pastor to participate in order to emphasize the seriousness of the situation and the depth of your concern.

In meeting #2 (with *your husband*): Your child could say, "Dad, last Friday when I brought a friend home, you were drunk on the couch. I felt so embarrassed. I love you and I want my friends to like you. It's so hard when I see the damage your drinking is doing."

Express genuine love and confidence in your husband. (See Ephesians 4:29–31.)

Although he may appear calloused, your husband probably fears rejection and wants to be accepted by you and your family. Share affirming statements like: "I love you. The reason I'm sharing these things with you is that I care. I know that with God's strength you can become the man you want to be." After each person has shared, one by one, some painful experience followed by reassurance of genuine care, the addict is often ready to receive help.

Have a practical plan ready to help your husband. (See Proverbs 24:11,12.)

Prior to the intervention:

- Contact a treatment facility and schedule an appointment for a time immediately after the confrontation.
- Review your insurance policies to determine whether this treatment will be covered.
- Review other financial documents such as bank statements.

- Contact your husband's employer to determine the status of his job if he goes into treatment.
- Be prepared to answer your husband's objections.
- Be ready to outline specific consequences if treatment is refused.

Choose to Be Content

I am not saying this because I am in need, for I have learned to be content whatever the circumstances (Philippians 4:11).

Place trust in your Provider. (See Psalm 9:10.)

Regardless of your husband's choices, choose to continue with your life.... Continue meeting each day with God, pouring out your heart and trusting His timing. As you allow the Lord to *be Lord* of your life, you will have the contentment of Christ.

See your spiritual family as your source of security. (See 1 John 3:1.)

Since you have experienced so much family pain—your heart has been hurt and trust has been trampled—insecurity is a natural result. But because your heavenly Father has placed you into His family, you can feel content—you are safe and secure. For when you are in His family, you are His child forever.

Allow others to help you "think healthy." (See Proverbs 16:16.)

Even if your husband refuses help, actively seek help for *yourself.* You need the support of others who understand what you're going through and who can compassionately help. Meet with a Christ-centered, biblical counselor or with support groups designed to help family members of alcoholics. Most of all, cling to the comfort and counsel that the Lord has for you.

Thank God for His goodness to you. (See Psalm 100:4,5.)

Focus on the good that God is doing in you and around you. Make a list of all the blessings for which you can thank Him. . . . Then take time to express your heart. A grateful spirit can produce contentment in any situation.

Love your husband with the love of the Lord. (See 2 Corinthians 1:3–5.)

During this time of trial, the more you draw on the love of God, the more love you will have for your husband. Pray this prayer: "Lord, may I love with Your love, be kind with Your kindness, and give comfort with Your comfort."

In your letter you said, "I don't know where to turn to for help." I encourage you to continue to look to the Lord—not as your helper, but as your *source of strength* and as your *resource for life.* With "Christ *in* you" (Colossians 1:27), you have the empowering presence of God for facing every problem. Never lose faith, for even when things seem impossible, "With God *all* things are possible" (Matthew 19:26)!

7

Codependency

Friendship Addiction

Dear June,

I left an emotionally dependent relationship which had started as a good friendship . . . but soon it became like an addiction . . . bad for you but hard to kick the habit. I consciously broke the routine and the pain was almost devastating. Now I find myself searching for the same emotional intensity I had with my friend. Can you give me some thoughts about how I can keep my friendships in focus?

Dear Frantic-for-Focus,

The candor of your letter was painful reading because recovery from an emotionally dependent relationship can be so difficult and deceiving. Until you deal with the root causes for forming emotionally dependent relationships, the cycle will be repeated again and again with one person and then another. Be aware that changing your patterns of relating to friends is a process which takes time, effort, and strong commitment. It will not be easy or painless but the outcome will mean freedom—the freedom to love and be loved within the boundaries of a healthy relationship.

Codependency is basically a relationship addiction. It is usually characterized by a weaker, dependent person who feels the *need to be connected* to a stronger person, while the stronger person feels the *need to be needed*. In reality, both people are insecure. What began as a constructive, joy-filled relationship results in a destructive cycle of manipulation and control that saps the joy and happiness out of life.

As you seek to conquer codependency, know that being raised in a dysfunctional family is often the cause of codependent behavior. Unfortunately, unhealthy patterns of trying to get inner needs met can be handed down from generation to generation. However, take heart—God is a God of new beginnings! To get *free* of your need for emotional intensity in a friendship, God gives you this hope: "Forget the former things; do not dwell on the past. See, I am doing a new thing!" (Isaiah 43:18,19).

Desire to Be Free

Recognize that your deepest dependency is on your friend instead of your Lord—which is part of modern-day idolatry.

> *You shall have no other gods before me* (Exodus 20:3).

- See how you emotionally "demand" that your friend meet your needs for love, significance, and security.

- Realize that God did not intend for you to meet all the needs of another person nor intend for another person to meet all of your needs. (Then neither of you would need God.)
- Admit that your codependency is a sin.
- Pray for God to give you the desire to please Him in all your relationships.

Deal with the Past

Since you haven't been able to get your inner needs met through past relationships and since you never will, extend forgiveness to those who have caused you pain.

> *Bear with each other and forgive whatever grievances you may have against one another. Forgive as the Lord forgave you* (Colossians 3:13).

- Reflect on any emotional or physical abuse you experienced as a child.
- Determine whom from your past you need to forgive.
- Understand the cause of the other person's manipulative or controlling behavior—expecting you to be their need-meeter.
- Choose to forgive each time your frustrating feelings come to the surface.

Discern Patterns of Codependence

Ask God to reveal your unhealthy patterns of relating so that you will know what needs to be changed.

Surely you desire truth in the inner parts; you teach me wisdom in the inmost place (Psalm 51:6).

- Do you believe that pleasing everyone is Christlike?
- Do you have difficulty being at peace if your friend is not at peace?
- Do you fear losing love if you allow your friend to suffer the consequences of negative actions?
- Do you say *yes* when you really believe you should say *no?*
- Do you seek to be your friend's "savior"?
- Do you feel you must make your friend be responsible?
- Do you feel you should always be in control of the relationship?
- Do you get easily angered when your friend disappoints or lets you down?
- Do you feel possessive of your friend's time and attention?
- Do you exclude others from the majority of your activities in order to be with your friend?

Declare Healthy Boundaries

Personal boundaries need to be established, communicated verbally, and *consistently* reinforced in order to break the codependency habit.

Above all else, guard your heart, for it is the wellspring of life (Proverbs 4:23).

- Communicate the need for change so you can work toward a healthly friendship.
- Write down and express your limits of responsibility and involvement.
- Seek outside help from a wise friend or counselor if you can't make headway.
- Maintain honest communication without using angry or abusive language.

Develop Spiritual Energy

Redirect your thoughts to the Lord.

> *Direct me in the path of your commands, for there I find delight* (Psalm 119:35).

- ✓ Make your relationship with the Lord and your spiritual growth your first priority.
- Nurture several close Christian friends, not just one.
- Become involved in helping other people.
- Attend a Bible study, read God's Word, and write down and memorize Galatians 1:10.

Discover Your Identity in Christ

When you are in Christ, you have a *new nature.*

> *Therefore, if anyone is in Christ, he is a new creation; the old has gone, the new has come!* (2 Corinthians 5:17).

- *Know the truth.* Because Christ lives in you, you have been set free.

  So if the Son sets you free, you will be free indeed (John 8:36).

- *Believe the truth.* Christ lives in you, providing the strength to do what you cannot do!

  I can do everything through him who gives me strength (Philippians 4:13).

- *Act on the truth.* Yield your natural desires to Christ and allow Him to determine your responses.

  You see that his [Abraham's] faith and his actions were working together, and his faith was made complete by what he did (James 2:22).

You must be congratulated on the wisdom and courage you have already shown by desiring and implementing change. While the Lord often expresses His love through others, He doesn't want you emotionally dependent on other people. He has given you three inner needs—unconditional love, significance, and security in order for you to realize that it is only through Him these needs can be completely met.

And my God will meet all your needs according to his glorious riches in Christ Jesus (Philippians 4:19).

8

Compulsive Eating

What's Eating You?

Dear June,

I have come to realize that my emotions and my overeating are tied together. I love to eat sweets and rich, fatty foods whenever I am tired, angry, stressed, happy, or sad. They make me feel able to cope. I have been on every diet that was ever printed and have lost and gained over 1000 pounds. I have been enslaved to food—especially sweets—for a number of years. I began to see it as sin a few years ago and have fought a little and failed a lot since then. One more time I will try to overcome this problem, but I need your prayers.

Dear Hungry for Healing,

How wise you are to realize that your compulsion to overeat has less to do with food than with the unmet needs you are attempting to fill. Hunger for food is not the real issue. What you are experiencing is a pervasive hunger to fill your *emotional plate* with something satisfying. Since the comfort of a cream pie lasts only minutes, it stands to reason that you would keep consuming everything from casseroles to cookies to cakes. But be sure of this, my friend, you *can* break this cycle of food frustration!

Check Your Thinking

Why do I want to keep eating?

When you are reaching for something to eat, stop! Consider *why* you want to eat. Ask yourself, "Am I really physically hungry or am I trying to satisfy some other emotional need?" If your body is hungry, eat; if your emotions are hungry, don't. Consider Proverbs 21:2, "All a man's ways seem right to him, but the LORD weighs the heart."

What needs am I trying to meet when I overeat?

In order to overcome compulsive eating, remind yourself that your behavior has an underlying purpose. You have three God-given inner needs: the need for unconditional love, for significance, and for security. God designed you in such a way that He alone would be able to meet those needs. Philippians 4:19 gives you this assurance, "My God will meet all your needs according to his glorious riches in Christ Jesus." As you know from experience, trying to fill your inner needs with a piled-up plate leads only to piled-up guilt. So ask God to show you the needs you're trying to satisfy with food rather than through Him. Pray: "Search me, O God, and know my heart; test me and know my anxious thoughts. See if there is any offensive way in me" (Psalm 139:23,24).

Evaluate what you are unconsciously saying to yourself:

- "I love food so much. When I eat, I feel *comforted* and *loved.*" *(the need for love)*
- "By controlling *what* I eat and *when* I eat, I am controlling my life, and that gives me some sense of significance." *(the need for significance)*
- "The inner satisfaction I get from feeling full makes me feel secure." *(the need for security)*

A full stomach can give you a sense of love, significance, and security—at least until you get hungry again! Then you plunge back into those hunger cravings. As you identify the *real need* behind your obsession for food, focus on God's provision to meet your need.

Do I use food to console myself regarding pain from the past or to escape my fear of the future?

Seek to get the most out of today. Don't dwell on yesterday's sorrow and don't live in fear of tomorrow. Live in the *present.* Rely on "Christ in you" (Colossians 1:27) to reveal His purpose for you. Let this be your vow: *"I will live for now."*

Am I comparing myself with how others look?

Second Corinthians 10:12 states that comparing is not wise: "When they measure themselves by themselves and compare themselves with themselves, they are not wise." Each time you are tempted to compare yourself to another person, remember that you are a precious and chosen child of God—regardless of your physical appearance. Thank God for how He sees you. First Samuel 16:7 says, "The LORD does not look at the things man looks at. Man looks at the outward appearance, but the LORD looks at the heart."

Change Your Behavior

Is my mind focused on what will help or hinder?

Read several nutrition books to *learn* more about good nutrition. Make a list of all the foods that are healthy and you can enjoy, then thank God for them. (English muffins and bagels are low in fat, while croissants, cornbread, and nutbreads are high in fat.) Instead of fixating on the foods you *shouldn't* eat, focus on the foods you *should* eat. Philippians 4:8 says, "Whatever is true, whatever is noble, whatever is right, whatever is pure, whatever is lovely, whatever is admirable—if anything is excellent or praiseworthy—think about such things."

Do I buy the wrong foods?

When grocery shopping, don't go to the store hungry and don't buy foods on impulse. Make a list of the healthy foods you need to buy, and then stick to your prepared list. Read nutrition labels and avoid foods with high fat content. (If you are craving sweets, try fruit, marshmallows, and most hard candies which have no fat—remember, chocolate and ice cream are high in fat.) Let Proverbs 5:23 provide your motivation, "He will die for lack of discipline, led astray by his own great folly."

Do I keep tempting foods around the house?

If your favorite no-no's aren't in your kitchen, you can't eat them. The source of temptation usually comes from within: "When tempted, no one should say, 'God is tempting me.' For God cannot be tempted by evil, nor does he tempt anyone; but each one is tempted when, by his own evil desire, he is dragged away and enticed" (James 1:13,14). So, don't keep fattening foods that tempt your tastebuds at home. Keep healthy snacks in easy reach for the time the next hunger pangs strike. (Raw vegetables, pretzels, and fruit make great snacks.)

What if I blow my diet?

Instead of thinking of yourself as being on a "diet," consider yourself as "eating healthy." Diets have an ending—usually *before* the desired results—followed by more weight gain than before. You can learn the habit of *eating healthy* as a way of life. However, if one evening you stuff and stuff until you puff, don't give up and go back to hiding overeating. Remember, the more you eat in secret, the less you can hide it openly! If you've been on a binge, realize that everyone has strayed off track at some time. Just get back on track the next meal—for Proverbs 25:16 gives this graphic caution, "If you find honey, eat just enough—too much of it, and you will vomit."

Am I getting the necessary exercise?

"Physical training is of some value" (1 Timothy 4:8). It is helpful in weight loss and good for your health. You can begin by taking a brisk twenty-minute walk once a day to increase your metabolism. While walking, memorize Scripture, pray, or visit with a friend. Personalize Scriptures such as Philippians 4:13: "I can *eat healthy today because of* him who gives me strength," "I can *walk twenty minutes today* through Christ who gives me strength." Other things you might consider doing include bicycling, swimming, aerobics, and even walking up stairs instead of riding on elevators.

Have I charted my emotions and eating habits?

Writing down what you eat and how you feel will help expose your habits—both good and bad. Get a notebook just for your food diary, and write down *everything* you eat. Do this faithfully for at least one week so you can see your eating patterns. In the end, you will be guilt-free when you have made this your priority: "Whether you eat or drink or whatever you do, do it all for the glory of God" (1 Corinthians 10:31).

Should I be accountable to someone?

Ask for a friend's help to keep you accountable. Share daily what you've eaten, how you've exercised, and how you're feeling. (You also may want to continue your food diary to help keep you accountable.) Pray for each other and "carry each other's burdens, and in this way you will fulfill the law of Christ" (Galatians 6:2).

Am I nurturing my relationship with God?

Because Jesus indwells you, pray throughout the day that your choices will reflect the character of Christ—specifically

His self-control—and read Romans 6 about how you are dead to sin's enslavement. Claim God's protection from and power over temptation, and thank Him for His faithfulness to you.

> No temptation has seized you except what is common to man. And God is faithful; he will not let you be tempted beyond what you can bear. But when you are tempted, he will also provide a way out so that you can stand up under it (1 Corinthians 10:13).

Am I wanting to lose weight for the right reason?

Why do you want to conquer this compulsion? So that you will look better? So that you will have more self-control? As good as these reasons are, they are self-focused and secondary. Your major motive for losing weight should be to please your Lord. Then you are no longer enslaved to self-indulgence—you are the Lord's "bond slave" and working to please Him. You should not change just because you have set a goal for yourself, but because that is His goal for you. As 2 Corinthians 5:9 says, "So we make it our goal to please Him. . . ."

How I want to encourage you—change is difficult, but doable! By acknowledging your need for change and your powerlessness to effect that change, you have taken the first step. If you are saying, "I don't have the willpower to resist the food that I love," be confident of this: *The issue is not the power of your will, but the power of your God.* As you rely on the Spirit of Christ within you, *He will change your focus for you.* Your focus will not be on food but on faith: faith that He will meet your emotional needs, faith that He will break your hunger habit, and faith that food will not be your god—God will be your God.

Amen.

Thank you Lord for this deliverance.

9

Homosexuality

Mistaken Identity

Dear June,

As a result of counseling that uncovered childhood sexual abuse, I am now dealing with my strong, exclusive attraction to other women. I feel like my life is a nightmare because even though I haven't acted out these desires, I feel so ashamed at what I am. I am a Christian, but fighting depression and the desire to end my life. I am so scared.

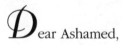

Dear Ashamed,

My heart ached when *I* read your letter because you are obviously broken over your situation. I admire your courage in writing so openly, and let me assure you that you are not alone! Feelings of hopelessness and depression are natural when something seems to have control over you—whether that something is stealing, lying, or one's sexual desires. But God knows how to bring healing and wholeness to your life. You will find comfort as you claim these promises from God:

> The LORD is close to the brokenhearted and saves those who are crushed in spirit (Psalm 34:18).
>
> He heals the brokenhearted and binds up their wounds (Psalm 147:3).

Understand the Connection Between Your Past and the Present

The attraction you feel toward other women is not unique for someone who has been sexually abused. In fact, sexual abuse victims often gravitate to one of three extremes: they may become heterosexually promiscuous, they may consider homosexuality as a lifestyle, or they may view themselves as totally asexual. I mention this so you'll understand that your emotions are not uncommon. But most important is what you *choose to believe* and how you *choose to act* in relation to your emotions.

What have you believed? Have you thought, *If God allowed me to be abused, then He must not love and care about me?* If so, then nothing could be further from the truth! Jesus, who suffered unjust humiliation and extreme physical abuse—instead of retaliating—entrusted Himself to God, the just judge. (See 1 Peter 2:19–23.) Likewise, entrust yourself to God, who hears your cry and who will judge those who hurt you. Even if those who were supposed to love you twisted that love, God will never do that. He will always be there for you. "Though my father and mother forsake me, the LORD will receive me" (Psalm 27:10).

Understand the Difference Between Temptation and Sin

Temptation is not sin. Even Jesus was tempted! Hebrews 4:15 says, "For we do not have a high priest who is unable to sympathize with our weaknesses, but we have one who has been tempted in every way, just as we are—yet was without sin." It's not the temptation that is wrong—it's what you *do* with the temptation.

Temptation's battleground is in your mind. If you are focusing on your attraction to other women, this may be why your "life is like a nightmare." The thoughts or desires which flash through your mind are uncontrollable many times, but what you *do* with them is not! Second Corinthians 10:5 tells you to "take captive every thought to make it obedient to Christ." That means continually dwelling on what is right in God's sight and consciously barricading your mind from the wrong. Specifically, the moment you have a tempting thought (which you will), replace that thought with these words, "Lord, whatever it takes to reflect the character of Christ who is in me, that's what I'm willing to do." Make this your constant prayer.

Temptation is resistible. You can trust God to keep the temptation from becoming so strong that you can't stand up against it. He has promised this, and He is always faithful to His promises.

> No temptation has seized you except what is common to man. And God is faithful; he will not let you be tempted beyond what you can bear. But when you are tempted, he will also provide a way out so that you can stand up under it (1 Corinthians 10:13).

Understand the Truth of Who You Really Are

Your identity is based on who you are in Christ. As an authentic Christian, redeemed and cleansed by the blood of Jesus Christ, you have a new God-given identity. Second Corinthians 5:17 says, "Therefore, if anyone is in Christ, he is a new creation; the old has gone, the new has come!" You have become the very righteousness of God (2 Corinthians 5:21). At salvation your old self died; now, when God looks at you, He sees Jesus.

The fact that your desires need to be redirected does not change who you are in Christ. You are a blood-bought believer who can boldly approach God's throne of grace without fear of condemnation. Resting in the knowledge that you are wholly loved and accepted by God, you can be sure God is at work within you to change your desires and complete the work He has started in you. "Being confident of this, that He who began a good work in you will carry it on to completion until the day of Jesus Christ" (Philippians 1:6).

Your desires can be changed because you have Christ in you *to do the changing*. Many people falsely believe the myth, "Once a homosexual, always a homosexual." Yet that is simply not true; there are many former homosexuals today who can attest to that fallacy. Even in the first century A.D. many homosexuals were set free through the power of Christ. First Corinthians 6:9–11 says,

> Neither the sexually immoral nor idolaters nor adulterers nor male prostitutes nor homosexual offenders nor thieves nor the greedy nor drunkards nor slanderers nor swindlers will inherit the kingdom of God. *And that is what some of you were.* But you were washed, you were sanctified, you were justified in the name of the Lord Jesus Christ and by the Spirit of our God (emphasis added).

In your letter you mentioned "the desire to end your life," but your situation is not hopeless! The Lord holds your future in His hands—a future full of hope. Jeremiah 29:11 says, " 'For I know the plans I have for you,' declares the LORD, 'plans to prosper you and not to harm you, plans to give you hope and a future.' " Be assured your life is very much worth living because you are very dear to God's heart. The Lord Himself declares, "You are precious and honored in my sight, and . . . I love you" (Isaiah 43:4). Most people who want to end their lives feel that way because they see no way of escape. But on the authority of the Word of God you can be set free!

Understand How to Be Free from Homosexual Feelings

Freedom never comes easily! History testifies that freedom is won only at great cost—which is often death. Freedom from the bondage of sin has the same price tag. God wants you to "die" to wanting to get your love needs met illegitimately. As you rely on "Christ in you" to meet your inner needs, you will win the war. "It is for freedom that Christ has set us free. Stand firm, then, and do not let yourselves be burdened again by a yoke of slavery" (Galatians 5:1).

Steps for Freedom

F*ace* the truth that homosexual behavior is a sin, forbidden by God (Romans 1:26,27).

R*ealize* that you have the Redeemer, Jesus Christ, who will set you free from sin (Luke 4:18).

E*xchange* your lack of control for Christ's control by yielding your body to Christ (Romans 6:11–14).

E*liminate* the belief that your willpower can set you free (John 15:5).

D*iscover* that in Christ you have a new identity with a new heart and new desires (Ezekiel 36:26,27).

O*pen* the door to healthy relationships and close the door on homosexual relationships (1 Corinthians 15:33,34).

M*aintain* an eternal perspective and a focus on godly priorities (Hebrews 12:1).

Write each of these passages on an index card, review them each day for six months, and commit them to memory.

Realize that if you see yourself as homosexual, yet you have Christ in you, you have a mistaken identity. Since the Bible says you are "transformed by the renewing of your mind," what you allow yourself to think is vitally important (see Romans 12:2). Right thought produces right action, and wrong thought produces wrong action. When you dwell on your true identity you have the empowering presence of Christ in you, finding expression through you. Then more and more every day you will mirror the moral character of Christ!

10

Phobias

Exchange Panic for Peace

Dear June,

I have been experiencing panic attacks. The last attack occurred while I was driving, and it could have been a very dangerous situation. I now have a fear of driving and a fear for the safety of those in the car with me. Negative thoughts occupy my mind most of the time. I am critical, worry a lot, and fear the worst. I need help in overcoming this problem.

Dear Panic-Stricken,

I hear your concern—you are feeling out of control. Yet you are wise to seek the help that you need. Rest assured, this frightening fear can be overcome instead of you being overcome!

Facts About Fear

Periodically, everyone experiences a *momentary, rational fear* of danger; however, you recognize that you're experiencing a persistent, irrational fear which could be called a *phobia.* Well, don't feel alone. One out of every nine people will have a phobia in his or her lifetime. A phobia is "an exaggerated, irrational fear" which most people do confront and overcome. Even those who have phobic disorders (phobias impairing normal functioning) can be set free. Take heart, there is liberating hope for you! The Lord says, "Fear not, for I have redeemed you; I have called you by name, you are mine" (Isaiah 43:1 RSV).

Facts About Feelings

Your own letter held the key to unlocking your prison door: Change your thinking! Change what you allow your mind to dwell on. Romans 12:2 states, "Be transformed by the renewing of your mind." Understand, *feeling follows thinking.* So when you change your thinking, your emotions change and your actions change. (If you *think* fearful thoughts, you will *feel* fearful and *act* fearful. Likewise, if your thoughts dwell on trusting God with your life, you will *feel* trusting and then *act* according to that trust.)

At this point you may be wondering, "How can I change my thinking?" Let me share three projects which I pray will release you from being held hostage to fear.

Focus on Your Protector

Your heavenly Protector never created you to be plagued with panic. Hear His heart toward you as He says, "Do not fear, for I am with you; do not be dismayed, for I am your God. I will strengthen you and help you; I will uphold you with my righteous right hand" (Isaiah 41:10).

Make this passage practical by writing your name on an index card followed by His scriptural promise. Then read it out loud several times morning, noon, and night every day for the next twelve weeks. Over time, as you personalize His promise, you will "be transformed by the renewing of your mind."

Other passages to memorize that will help develop your trust in God's constant presence and protection are:

Psalm 46:1,2	Proverbs 3:25,26
Psalm 56:3,4	Isaiah 41:13
Psalm 91:2	Lamentations 3:57
Proverbs 1:33	Zephaniah 3:15

Focus on Your Shepherd

What do you do if you feel a panic attack beginning? Let me suggest that you keep with you at all times a copy of Psalm 23, or better yet, memorize it. This psalm is considered by many to be the best loved Scripture in the Bible. When the fingers of fear begin to strangle your feelings, personalize these six short verses of Psalm 23.

Verse 1: Immediately picture the presence of your Shepherd. Breathe deeply and say slowly, "The Lord is *my* shepherd . . . the Lord is my *shepherd* . . ." Do this ten times, emphasizing a different word each time. (Practice this now and notice the peace that comes.)

Verse 2: Move deliberately to a still, quiet place. Think about verse two, "He makes me lie down in green pastures, He leads me beside quiet waters."

Verse 3: Take ten more deep breaths, each time repeating "He *restores* my soul."

✓**Verse 4**: Know that you aren't trapped in this valley . . . you are *just passing through*. Repeat confidently ten times, "I will fear no evil—the Lord is with me."

Verse 5: See how He prepares you to move past your "enemy" which is the fear He has already defeated.

Verse 6: Thank God for the way He will use this experience for *good* in your life . . . by drawing you into a deeper dependence on Him. Good will "follow you" because later you will be able to reach out with a heart of compassion to other people who are confined by their fears.

Let the Lord use the twenty-third psalm as part of your healing process. After all, God designed His Word to be used for healing: "He sent forth his word and healed them" (Psalm 107:20). The practical application of this comforting pastoral psalm is that, if you focus on your fear, your panic will increase, but if you focus on your Shepherd, your fearfulness will cease.

Face Your Fear

Most people with phobias eventually realize that their excessive fear is not fear of an object (like cats) or a situation (like heights). Their deepest fear is that *they will display an out-of-control response*. Thus, for you to regain control and confidence in driving, you will receive immense help by going through the process of "desensitization," which simply means to *gradually* increase your exposure to what you fear. I suggest you ask a trustworthy, supportive friend to walk with you slowly through each of these steps. Don't rush the process. You may need to spend days or even weeks on each step before progressing to the next step.

- For several days focus on pleasant pictures of people who are driving. (Perhaps get pictures from car dealerships or magazines.) As you look at the pictures, claim Philippians 4:13, "I can do everything through him who gives me strength."
- Go to a busy street, watch the flow of traffic, and claim the truth of Proverbs 1:33, "Whoever listens to me will live in safety and be at ease, without fear of harm."
- Repeatedly slide into the driver's seat of your car and turn on the engine . . . each time claiming 2 Timothy 1:7, "God did not give [me] a spirit of timidity, but a spirit of power, of love and of self-discipline."
- Drive around the block claiming Deuteronomy 31:8, "The LORD himself goes before you and will be with you; he will never leave you nor forsake you. Do not be afraid; do not be discouraged."
- Then venture out on a longer route claiming Psalm 34:4, "He delivered me from all of my fears."

Don't be overwhelmed by all these steps . . . *just take them one at a time*. Remember, the longest journey begins with a single step.

Many years ago President Franklin Roosevelt said, "The only thing we have to fear is fear itself." Yet, you don't have to be fearful of fear! If you have received the Lord Jesus Christ into your heart you have "Christ in you" (Colossians 1:27) to be the Prince of Peace for you. Because He *is* perfect love and in you, He will exchange your panic for peace.

Perfect love drives out fear (1 John 4:18).

Part 3

Agony of Abuse

11

Sexual Abuser

VICTORY FOR THE VIOLATOR

Dear June,

When I was about five, my cousin sexually abused me. When I was seven, a boy sexually abused me in a bathroom. I later abused another boy for a while. One night with a pounding in my heart, I went to my parents and began to work through my past. I am in a Christian environment and getting Christian counseling. I am fourteen and have a close relationship with Jesus, but I need prayer very badly for this battle.

Dear Warrior,

It took great courage for you to share such personal and painful events in your life. You are certainly to be commended for recognizing your need for help and then pursuing that help both through your parents and through Christian counseling. Living a life pleasing to God is not easy for anyone. It is a continuing challenge to maintain godliness, dedication, and obedience. You obviously are determined to overcome life's difficulties. But when you are pinned down by the effects of sexual abuse, either as a victim or a perpetrator, those difficulties are greatly intensified.

However—no battle is too difficult for God to win! Through His Spirit living in you and His Word written for you, He provides *every* weapon you need to live a victorious life. The following truths will help you become the conquering hero that God has created you to be.

Claim Your New Freedom

When you became a Christian, you enlisted in God's army and received a new heart from the Commanding General! He made you new at the very core of your being so that your attitudes and actions could become more and more like Christ's. "If anyone is in Christ, he is a new creation; the old has gone, the new has come!" (2 Corinthians 5:17). Christ has freed you from the enemy's influence so that you might fight the good fight for the Lord. He has given you freedom!

Freedom from the Penalty of Sin

When you first came to God to confess your sins and your need of a Savior, God completely cleansed you, forgave you, and marked off your war crimes as paid in full. "If we confess our sins, he is faithful and just and will forgive us our sins and purify us from all unrighteousness" (1 John 1:9). God forgave your crimes of sexual abuse.

Freedom from the Power of Sin

Before you became a Christian you were controlled by sin—*the enemy's forces*—operating in you. Then, when you became a Christian, you entered into *Christ's victory over those forces.* Simply put, because you are in Christ and because He soundly defeated sin at the cross, *you,* too, have victory over sin. It's not that you can't sin—you can still *choose* to sin, but you are no longer *controlled* by sin. Sin's power is broken. "Our old self was crucified with him so that the body of sin might be [rendered powerless], that we should no longer be slaves to sin" (Romans 6:6). You no longer need to be tempted or controlled by improper sexual urges.

Freedom from the Guilt of Sin

Guilt can be either good or bad. Good guilt comes from the Holy Spirit within you as He convicts you of attitudes and actions which displease Him. He puts a heaviness on your heart persuading you to confess your wrongs and then He enables you to change your wrongs and make them right. This is what led you to confess your crimes, and we praise God for this type of guilt!

Bad guilt occurs when, even after you have changed, you still feel condemned and consumed by guilt. (See "Guilt" under Part 1.) According to the Bible, you received a merciful gift from God because you are in Christ (a Christian) and you will never be condemned by God. "There is now no condemnation for those who are in Christ Jesus" (Romans 8:1). I pray you will not be overrun by this type of guilt. If you have genuinely grieved over your sin and turned from it—as difficult as it may be for you to imagine—your sin is totally forgiven by God. You no longer have to carry any burden of guilt from the past. "Your guilt is taken away and your sin atoned for" (Isaiah 6:7).

Freedom to Seek the Forgiveness of Others

But along with your new freedoms come new responsibilities. You wrote that you had abused another boy "for a while" which leads me to believe that this behavior belongs to the past—that you have not only changed your actions, but also your attitudes. These changes are commendable. However, how do you think your past actions have affected *his* life? He could very well be in as much pain as you, or even more.

With your parents and your counselor, prayerfully consider contacting this boy and asking for his forgiveness. Perhaps, as a Christian, you will be the instrument that begins the healing process in *his* life. This is also your biblical responsibility. "If you are offering your gift at the altar and there remember that your brother has something against you, leave your gift there in front of the altar. First go and be reconciled to your brother; then come and offer your gift" (Matthew 5:23,24).

Freedom to Forgive Others

The instant you became a true Christian, you received the very life of Christ—"Christ in you" (Colossians 1:27). By receiving His life, you also received His strength—"I can do everything through him who gives me strength" (Philippians 4:13). Therefore, whatever God tells you to do (such as forgive),

He will give you the strength to do it. Have you ever forgiven your cousin and the boy who abused you? If not, the Bible says, "Bear with each other and forgive whatever grievances you may have against one another. Forgive as the Lord forgave you" (Colossians 3:13).

It is easier to forgive others when you realize how much Christ has forgiven you! Choosing to forgive means *not* demanding that your cousin or the other boy "pay" for what they did to you. You release them from that obligation just as you would forgive a financial debt.

If you do *not* choose to forgive these boys, you hurt only yourself. Unforgiveness will produce a bitter heart—in you. So, by letting go of your desire for revenge, you set yourself free from bondage to your own bitterness.

Freedom to Confront in Love

Once you have conquered in the battle to forgive your abusers, it may be time to confront them. Again, with the help of your counselor, make the effects of their actions known to both of these boys. Remember, you may be the only Christian in this battle, and you *need to try* to save the lives of others. "Remember this: Whoever turns a sinner from the error of his way will save him from death and cover over a multitude of sins" (James 5:20).

Claim Your New Power

Are your sinful sexual urges still bombarding you with negative thoughts? Typically, your *thoughts* and *actions* today are born out of the patterns you established yesterday. Those patterns could have been good or bad. If your past patterns were negative ones, God can renew your mind, transform your thinking, and thoroughly break their influence on you.

In its proper place—marriage—sex can be a wonderful gift designed by God for a couple's mutual enjoyment. All thoughts and actions outside of that context are sinful. Improper thoughts and actions will form negative patterns which develop into strongholds in your life. This is what has happened to you.

Sexual strongholds are broken down only by renewing your mind. The Bible explains, "Do not conform any longer to the pattern of this world, but be transformed by the renewing of your mind" (Romans 12:2). But how is your mind renewed? Simply put, your mind is renewed when you replace the enemy's lies with God's perfect truth. That truth, of course, is found only in God's Word, the Bible.

According to Ephesians 6:17, the Bible is your sword for the battle. So, when you think a bad thought, draw your sword! God's pure thoughts defeat Satan's vile thoughts every time. "How can a young man keep his way pure? By living according to your word. . . . I have hidden your word in my heart that I might not sin against you" (Psalm 119:9,11).

Your key strategies for victory will be found in the pages of your Bible. Start with Philippians 4:13, "I can do everything through him who gives me strength." Uncover other meaningful verses, write them out on index cards, and put them in prominent places (like on your bathroom mirror). Read them until they are committed to memory, then, when sinful thoughts attack, *draw your sword!* For example, if a sinful sexual thought invades your mind, pull out your sword and slay it with 1 Thessalonians 4:7: "God did not call us to be impure, but to live a holy life."

You are no longer a prisoner of your past sin patterns. God has not left you to fight this battle alone. His presence and strength equip you for fighting with:

His provision: "God is faithful; he will not let you be tempted beyond what you can bear. But when you are tempted, he will also provide a way out so that you can stand up under it" (1 Corinthians 10:13).

His presence: "The LORD your God goes with you; he will never leave you nor forsake you" (Deuteronomy 31:6).

His power: "I can do everything through him who gives me strength" (Philippians 4:13).

His promises: "Your kingdom is an everlasting kingdom, and your dominion endures through all generations" (Psalm 145:13).

When you are tempted by sexual thoughts and actions not pleasing to God, call on Christ for His strength to resist. Remember—Jesus has already gained victory over sin—it is *His* victory parade you will one day walk in.

Claim Your New Purpose

Do you know you are important to God's great battle plan? He created you for specific assignments, and nothing has happened that can thwart His plans for you. Trust Him as He takes care of every strategic move: "'For I know the plans I have for you,' declares the LORD 'plans to prosper you and not to harm you, plans to give you hope and a future'" (Jeremiah 29:11). You may not understand why such painful events have happened to you, but rest assured that none of your life is wasted when you place it into the hands of your heavenly Commander-in-Chief.

Claim Your New Life

Asking for help is a difficult step in the battle strategy for healing. Since you have shared your hurts with your parents, a counselor, and with me, that part is behind you. Now you must face new battles—like forgiveness and confrontation—but rest assured that God will see you through these skirmishes as well.

✓Making the right decisions for your life is difficult, but making them is essential to ensure your ultimate victory. You are engaged in a spiritual war over your mind, your will, and your emotions. It is imperative that you utilize all of the artillery God provides for your triumph.

> For our struggle is not against flesh and blood, but against the rulers, against the authorities, against the powers of this dark world and against the spiritual forces of evil in the heavenly realms. Therefore put on the full armor of God, so that when the day of evil comes, you may be able to stand your ground, and after you have done everything, to stand (Ephesians 6:12–13).

Your Assignments in God's Battle Plan

- Keep your focus on Jesus (Hebrews 12:1,2)
- Pray daily for His protection (Psalm 28:7)
- Fill your mind with His Word (Psalm 119:147)
- Stay accountable to your parents and counselor (Proverbs 1:8,9)
- Look to the Lord for direction (Psalm 32:8)

Above all, your highest priority is to implement a close relationship with Jesus Christ! As you look to Him and let Him fight for you, you will experience victory in any area of your life you choose to attack.

> *The LORD your God is the one who goes with you to fight for you against your enemies to give you victory* (Deuteronomy 20:4).

12

Victim Mentality

Prisoner of the Past

Dear June,

As a child I was secretly sexually invaded. I'm not sure, but I think those incidents play a significant part in my low self-esteem and feelings of being controlled by circumstances and people. I feel so helpless.

I am 24 years old, a single mother of two, with one on the way. I feel very guilty about my sin. My father is an ordained minister and very disappointed in me, but he doesn't make me feel as bad as my mom and sister do.

The burden to come out from under this confused, unhappy, tumultuous way of life is tremendous. I've asked Jesus into my heart, so why can't I grasp the answer to my needs?

Dear Controlled,

The pain you have endured over the years has obviously been devastating and continues to weigh heavily on your mind and heart. Nothing has such far-reaching and long-term effects as childhood sexual abuse. In your letter you wrote, "I've asked Jesus into my heart, so why can't I grasp the answer to my needs?" With this in mind, I would like to share a few insights with you which will begin to free you from your "prison" of powerlessness.

Prisoner of the Past

When a child is being sexually abused, the child is powerless. Feeling out of control is natural when being violated by someone (either physically, mentally, or emotionally). As a result of the violation and being powerless to stop it, several unspoken and unconscious beliefs are formed. Those beliefs begin to determine your choices and dictate your actions and ultimately shape your life. One of those beliefs is that *others have the power to control you*—that you are powerless. Another belief is that *there is something innately wrong with you*—that you are a bad person and deserve bad things to happen to you.

After the actual victimization has stopped, this sense of powerlessness continues to permeate your very being. This is referred to as "victim mentality." You are no longer a victim, but you keep acting like a victim. Tragically, and all too often, this victim mentality is carried into adulthood which is profoundly detrimental to your relationships with others.

You have begun to realize that, even though you have accepted Jesus, your emotional life is still a prisoner to your past. That is why it is necessary to face the truth fully about the past so that you can move forward in freedom—free from fear, free from being controlled, free to feel your God-given worth.

Freedom from the Past

Face the Prisoner

If you feel powerless in relationships, have difficulty trusting others, and feel there is no way out of your problems, you are a prisoner of your past. The first step to freedom is facing the fact that you are not emotionally free, that you are in bondage, and that God doesn't want you staying in that prison any longer. The Lord knows how to release your repressed feelings. Trust Him to set the emotional captive free. "Trust in the LORD with all your heart and lean not on your own understanding; in all your ways acknowledge him, and he will make your paths straight" (Proverbs 3:5,6). Pray, "Lord, I admit that at times I feel controlled, that . . ."

Face the Past

Remembering is vital to healing. If memories of the abuse have been blocked, when they begin to return the first memories will be the *fact* of being abused. Then *specific details* of the abuse will begin to emerge. The most difficult stage will be remembering your *emotional response* at the time of your abuse. Consequently, you may need to seek the help of a Christ-centered biblical counselor in dealing with these memories. "Surely you desire truth in the inner parts; you teach me wisdom in the inmost place" (Psalm 51:6).

Face Your Pain

Ask Christ for the courage to relive the painful emotions of your past. Though you may think you will never be healed, take heart, for you can get past the hurt—

- by clinging to the promises of God.

  My comfort in my suffering is this: Your promise preserves my life (Psalm 119:50).

- by casting your burden on the Lord.

  Praise be to the Lord, to God our Savior, who daily bears our burdens (Psalm 68:19).

- by renewing your mind.

  Do not conform any longer to the pattern of this world, but be transformed by the renewing of your mind. Then you will be able to test and approve what God's will is—his good, pleasing and perfect will (Romans 12:2).

Face Your Private Secret

Keeping your abuse a secret only keeps you chained to the past. The power of the "secret" must be broken by bringing it out into the open. Begin sharing your painful past with a wise and trusted friend. Like taking care of a festering wound—as painful as it is—get the sinful secret out so there can be cleansing and healing. "But whoever lives by the truth comes into the light, so that it may be seen plainly that what he has done has been done through God" (John 3:21).

Face God's Permission

Be honest with God and admit your anger about what happened to you. Ephesians 4:26 says "In your anger do not sin." Trust Him with your feelings and go to Him with honest questions, such as:

> *"Where were You when this happened?"*
>
> *Answer:* Nothing catches God by surprise.
>
> > The eyes of the Lord are everywhere, keeping watch on the wicked and the good (Proverbs 15:3).
>
> *"Why haven't You punished my offender?"*
>
> *Answer:* God will avenge the innocent in His own time and in His own way.
>
> > A little while, and the wicked will be no more; though you look for them they will not be found. . . . For the power of the wicked will be broken, but the LORD upholds the righteous (Psalm 37:10, 17).
>
> *"If You love me, how could You have allowed this to happen?"*
>
> *Answer:* God does allow unjust suffering, but in doing so, He uses evil to bring about good results.
>
> > ✓And we know that in all things God works for the good of those who love him, who have been called according to his purpose (Romans 8:28).

Face the Pardon

You were used and abused, yet God says you are to forgive. God does not ask you to forgive the offense, only the offender. "Bear with each other and forgive whatever grievances you may have against one another. Forgive as the Lord forgave you" (Colossians 3:13). Why should you? After all, *you* were the victim. Because forgiveness frees you from staying a victim. For deeper offenses, forgiveness is not a one-time act. It is a *process* of forgiving again and again.

Face the Perpetrator

Confrontation is best done when you have had a period of separation from the offender and when you can confront positively and in strength. Proverbs 12:18 says, "Reckless words pierce like a sword, but the tongue of the wise brings healing." Why confront if it was a long time ago? Confrontation is a biblical principle, "If your brother sins against you, go and show him his fault, just between the two of you. If he listens to you, you have won your brother over" (Matthew 18:15). Confrontation can be used by God to convict the offender of sin and to promote your personal healing.

Face Your Patterns of Behavior

Since God created you with inner needs for love, significance, and security, look at what you have been doing to get your inner needs met. Have you had difficulty saying no, trying to *earn love?* Have you put projects over people trying to *look significant?* Have you excessively clung to someone trying to *feel secure?* Maybe you have already realized that your own attempts come up empty.

The answer to these deepest longings is to look to the Lord for fulfillment. He wants to be your Need-Meeter. When you know how much the Lord loves you, you will be less needy for the love of others. When you see how significant you are to Him, you won't need to seek others to supply your self-worth. When you see how secure you are as His child, the less you will look for security from others. Philippians 4:19 will become true to you: "And my God will meet all your needs according to his glorious riches in Christ Jesus." Ultimately, when you let the Lord meet your needs He will make you whole. And then you will be free to interact with others, not out of neediness but out of wholeness.

You have the very presence of Almighty God living inside you to heal you from the pain of the past. You have "Christ in you" (Colossians 1:27) as your source of strength to admit the abuse, to help with healing, to process the pain, to forgive the offender, and to face the future. You don't have to be a prisoner. His empowering presence means you have the *mind of Christ* to unchain the victim mentality and *set you free.*

> *If the Son sets you free, you will be free indeed* (John 8:36).

13

Manipulation

The Number One Guilt Game

Dear June,

My mother is a manipulative type of person. I have been feeling very guilty that I cannot fulfill the expectations that she has. I feel hopeless at times. I try to make her happy and satisfy her emotional needs . . . yet I can't. I have often felt angry and afraid. I have lied to her in an attempt to patch up the relationship. . . . When I am at college, I am satisfied, confident, and full of joy . . . but as soon as I come home, I fall back into patterns of guilt, submission, and childish anger.

Dear Guilt-Jerked,

How well you describe the many symptoms of being manipulated. You seem to have been led to believe that you *can* and *must* meet all your mother's needs. However, that is not your calling from God! Consider this: If you were to meet *all* of her needs then wouldn't you be taking the role that God alone should have? In reality, meeting all your mother's needs is a role that God alone can fill. It is an impossible task for you because you are not God.

Your mother, as well as each of us, has three God-given inner needs—a need for unconditional love, for significance, and for security. God designed us with these basic needs so we would ultimately look to Him and depend on Him for fulfillment. While He will work through you, through others, and through circumstances to meet some of your mother's needs, you are not to be the *source* for meeting all of her needs. God wants to be her Need-Meeter. So, if you met all your mother's needs then she wouldn't really need the Lord, would she? No. So for the sake of your mother's spiritual and emotional state, don't allow yourself to be fettered by false guilt (see "Guilt" under Part 1). Once you begin to establish proper boundaries with your mother, God will begin a healing work in both of your lives. Prayerfully, your mother will begin to depend on the Lord for her inner needs. By learning to recognize her methods of control, you can begin to maneuver out of manipulation into honest communication and a more healthy relationship with your mother.

Marks of Manipulation

How do you recognize that you are being manipulated? Several common characteristics are present in many relationships. Let me encourage you to get honest with your feelings and examine your relationship with your mother (and others) while answering the following questions.

Do You Feel Guilty?

***You may have* false guilt.**

True guilt is a *fact* . . . the result of realizing that you have been wrong, that you have sinned. False guilt is a *feeling* . . . the result of blaming yourself although you haven't sinned or continuing to blame yourself for a wrong after you have confessed and turned from your sin. False guilt often comes from failing to meet *another person's* expectations, *not God's* expectations. Galatians 1:10 tells us to please God: "Am I now trying to win the approval of men, or of God? Or am I trying to please men? If I were still trying to please men, I would not be a servant of Christ."

Do You Feel Responsible?

***You may have* repressed anger.**

If you feel responsible for your mother's lack of happiness, security, or sense of significance, she could be "blame shifting"—not taking personal responsibility for her own actions and blaming you for her problems. If so, you probably feel anger toward her. What is the truth in this situation? You can't be the source of anyone's happiness or security—after all, you won't always be available. *The Lord must be her source.* So what is God's perspective? Each person is responsible for his or her own actions and attitudes as stated in Galatians 6:7,8: "Do not be deceived: God cannot be mocked. A man reaps what he sows. The one who sows to please his sinful nature, from that nature will reap destruction; the one who sows to please the Spirit, from the Spirit will reap eternal life."

Do You Feel Rejected?

***You may be receiving* performance-based acceptance.**

When you do not act or respond as your mother wishes, she may use rejection (using tactics from silent treatment to sarcasm to screaming) to gain what she wants from you. If that is the case, then her acceptance of you is "performance-based"—based on what you *do* rather than on who you *are*. Remember *you are precious to God* and He accepts you just as you are: "But now he has reconciled you by Christ's physical body through death to present you *holy in his sight, without blemish and free from accusation*" (Colossians 1:22, emphasis added).

Do You Feel Indebted?

***You may have a* fear of disapproval.**

This is what I call "The Should Syndrome." Often it is expressed in these ways:

- "You *should* show me respect" (meaning, you *owe* me).
- "You *should* meet my needs" (meaning, you *ought* to).
- "You *should* make me happy" (meaning, I *expect* you to).
- "You *should* give me security" (meaning, you are *supposed* to).

Understand, you are not to live for the approval of others. Instead, rest in the security of God's unconditional love and acceptance. "Fear of man will prove to be a snare, but whoever trusts in the LORD is kept safe" (Proverbs 29:25).

Maneuvering Out of Manipulation

Once you recognize that you are allowing yourself to be manipulated, you can start to change the way you respond to your mother. Below are some steps to help you begin to develop a healthier and more honest way of communicating.

Choose to please the Lord first.

Decide to quit being a "people pleaser" and prioritize pleasing the Lord.

> So we make it our goal to please him, whether we are at home in the body or away from it (2 Corinthians 5:9).

Commit Galatians 1:10 to memory.

Write this verse on an index card and read it at least three times a day. When you are tempted to give in to a manipulative tactic or you begin to think the effort to withstand it is not worth it, replace that tempting thought with this verse:

> Am I now trying to win the approval of men, or of God? Or am I trying to please men? If I were still trying to please men, I would not be a servant of Christ (Galatians 1:10).

Cease your codependency.

Consider which of *your own* basic needs are being met through the relationship with your mother.

Dad ✓ *Do you need her constant approval to feel* loved?
✓ *Are you feeling* significant *by meeting all her needs?*
Do you sometimes lie to try to make her feel secure?

Remember, God desires to meet your own needs as well as those of your mother.

> And my God will meet all your needs according to his glorious riches in Christ Jesus (Philippians 4:19).

Challenge her unrealistic expectations.

✓ You are not responsible for meeting all of the needs of another person. Some of your mother's expectations may be realistic, but others are not. Determine your own priorities and responsibilities, then seek to do what the Lord leads you to do for your mother.

> A prudent man sees danger and takes refuge, but the simple keep going and suffer for it (Proverbs 22:3).

Count on difficulty.

Change can bring pain, so prepare yourself for pain. Just as change will be hard for you, it will be even more difficult for your mother. Expect her to experiment with different strategies or attempt to control you with anger.

> Endure hardship as discipline; God is treating you as sons. For what son is not disciplined by his father? (Hebrews 12:7).

Communicate truth in love.

Begin to respond lovingly but honestly to your mother. Notify your mother of the need for relating differently. You could say, "I haven't been responding to you in the most healthy way. I ask for your forgiveness. Instead of often responding out of fear, I want to respond to you out of truth." Do not become defensive or accept the blame if she falsely accuses you. Respectfully communicate your own feelings and then encourage her to do the same.

> The wise in heart are called discerning, and pleasant words promote instruction (Proverbs 16:21).

Do you sometimes feel guilty if you're not pleasing someone because you believe that, as a Christian, you should try to please everyone? Well, if you really want to be Christlike remember that Jesus did not please everyone. Many times He took an unpopular stand even with those closest to Him. He at times said "no" to others so that He could say "yes" to His Father.

Jesus was not a "people pleaser" but a "Father pleaser." He placed His dependence on His Father and focused on their relationship. Then, as He lived out of His Father's resources, He was used by His Father to meet the needs of others.

If you are to be Christlike, you must give up trying to be a "people pleaser" and focus on being a "Christ pleaser." God has not enabled you to please everyone, but He has enabled you to please Him. As you make pleasing Him your goal, you will then be free to be used by Him in meeting the needs of others . . . without being manipulated. And instead of being guilt-jerked you can now be *guilt-free!*

14

Wife Abuse

Used and Abused

Dear June,

I hope you can help me. My husband left me, and I didn't try to stop him because he was physically and emotionally abusive. If we had not separated, someone would have gotten hurt because of his violence. Now he says he wants to come home. I know I need to forgive him, but can't I forgive him without living with him? He continues to threaten me and my family, and I am very afraid. Does God really want me to live in an abusive situation?

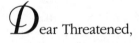

Dear Threatened,

How heartbreaking to hear of the degrading abuse you have suffered. Confusion, depression, and fear are normal and understandable for anyone who experiences these difficult circumstances. Although you may not feel a great deal of hope right now, the Word of God assures you that there is hope. Most importantly, as you seek to honor God and to keep you and your family safe, be sure you clearly understand God's heart and the biblical principles that apply to your abusive situation.

Abuse Is a Sin

God *never* wants you to be abused. Psalm 11:5 says, "The LORD examines the righteous, but the wicked and *those who love violence* his soul hates" (emphasis added). God never excuses or makes allowances for sin, nor does He want you to do so. Would yielding to your husband's inappropriate behavior demonstrate a godly response to evil? Of course not! God does not command you to obey or enable your husband's sinful actions. You can still maintain a godly love toward your husband while taking action to stop his abuse. God's Word makes it clear that your husband's inappropriate behavior should not be obeyed, condoned, or allowed. In fact, God commands you to submit to the government and its laws. Consider Romans 13:1–3,5:

> Everyone must submit himself to the governing authorities, for there is no authority except that which God has established. The authorities that exist have been established by God. Consequently, he who rebels against the authority is rebelling against what God has instituted, and those who do so will bring judgment on themselves.... Therefore, it is necessary to submit to the authorities, not only because of possible punishment but also because of conscience.

Physical abuse is not only a sin, it is against the law. The laws of both God and man require people to be accountable for inappropriate, illegal, sinful behavior.

Submission Is Often Misunderstood

Often women confuse the concept of biblical submission with obedience. In marriage, submission is an act of love which glorifies God. It is an *attitude of respect* toward authority which honors God. Yet biblical love, honor, and submission sometimes appear to be exactly the opposite of the world's definitions. For example, a wife who has the police arrest her alcoholic husband for driving while intoxicated may *appear* to be highly unsubmissive, disrespectful, and dishonoring to him. Yet that act could be one of the most loving and honoring things she could ever do for him. She is acting with *agape love,* seeking his highest good regardless of his response. Rather than allowing herself and others to be victims of his inappropriate behavior and rather than being angry, bitter, or rebellious, her heart is yielded before God and man. Biblical submission is an *attitude of the heart* from which loving (although sometimes tough) actions flow.

Confrontation Is Biblical

Biblical confrontation does not cause hurt or broken relationships. The hurt and the damage to relationships are the *result of sinful actions.* All sins have abiding consequences which remain even after the sin is forgiven. If your husband can continue to live a lifestyle of sin without facing the harm his actions cause, then he is being rescued from the natural consequences which *should* result from his sin. Rescuing an abuser from the consequences of sin is not helping him, is not loving him, nor is it in his best interest. "A hot-tempered man must pay the penalty; if you rescue him, you will have to do it again" (Proverbs 19:19).

On the other hand, biblical confrontation is loving and honoring to the abuser. It is an invitation for the person to face the reality of his sin and the harm it has caused so that he might choose to repent and be reconciled in his relationships with God and people. Remember, only after the prodigal son was forced to face the consequences of his sins did he repent. Biblical confrontation, although painful, is an act of love and honor toward those for whom you care. Since many people have been helped with Christ-centered biblical counseling, you might seek the assistance of someone trained in dealing with abusive relationships.

Separation Is an Option

In abusive situations, an indefinite separation is sometimes necessary until the abusive spouse repents and both parties have successfully completed both individual and marriage counseling. The desirable goals of separation are:

- To provide protection and safety for you and your family
- To force the offending spouse to face the consequences of his sin so that his hardened heart would be broken and he would truly repent

- To allow time for you to realistically face the damage the abuse caused and work through your resulting feelings in an honest and straightforward manner in order to move toward forgiveness and healing
- To reconcile the marriage

✓ Remember, the goal of separation is never divorce, but always reconciliation. Read 1 Corinthians 7:10,11. "A wife must not separate from her husband. But if she does, she must remain unmarried or else be *reconciled* to her husband" (emphasis added). mom

Truth Is Essential

The words and actions of an abusive spouse are often twisted and deceptive, so let me encourage you to be alert to the lies you may have believed as a result of your past and current circumstances. One of the most complex characteristics of abusive and controlling people is that they often incorporate bits of truth in their attacks. However, the truth is usually distorted, exaggerated, and combined with false conclusions. Therefore, it is important to discern the lies you may be believing. Ask yourself these questions to help differentiate fact from fiction in your situation.

- When I do not behave or respond as my husband wants, am I filled with the feeling of false guilt or fear? (False guilt comes from failing to meet man's expectations, not God's expectations, see "Guilt" under Part 1.)

- When I do not act or respond as my husband wants, do I feel belittled? Ridiculed? Rejected? What do I believe about myself? Do I believe that I am bad or somehow inadequate? Does God view me this way?
- Do I feel that I owe my husband? Do I feel ungrateful if I do not act in accordance with his wishes? Does he use phrases such as "you should" or "I expect you to . . ."? When he uses such phrases, do I feel guilty or bad? Is this the truth about how God sees me? What does God desire of me?
- Do I feel responsible for my husband's happiness or unhappiness, success or failure, reputation or standing in the community? Do I feel that he may be "blame shifting"—placing blame on me without taking personal responsibility for his own actions? What is the truth in this situation? What is God's perspective?
- Do I let my husband take the role in my life that God alone should have? Do I feel he claims absolute control and authority with no provision for appeal or compromise?

If the answer to any of these questions is yes, Stop! Immediately assess the situation. Remember, your strength and security come from God, not from another person. With the guidance and strength of the Holy Spirit, you can see the truth from God's perspective. Always keep your focus on God and His will for you, rather than on some other person and what expectations or demands they place on you. Galatians 1:10 says: "Am I now trying to win the approval of men, or of God? Or am I trying to please men?

If I were still trying to please men, I would not be a servant of Christ." It is helpful to know that people tend to abuse others out of fear and the need to feel powerful—but real power comes in knowing truth and acting on truth. Choose by an act of your will to depend on God and to stand in the strength of His truth. "Then you will know the truth, and the truth will set you free" (John 8:32).

Forgiveness Is Required

God wants to heal you—to truly transform you from the inside out. He doesn't put Band-Aids on deep wounds. Instead, He will root out the hurt from the depths of your heart so that His abundant life can flow where there once was only pain. You mentioned that you know that God wants you to forgive your husband. I am so glad that you want to do this because choosing to forgive is the beginning of the healing process. Before you can forgive, it will help you to understand exactly what forgiveness is *not*.

- Forgiveness is not a feeling, but a decision.
- Forgiveness is not always forgetting.
- Forgiveness is not denying or minimizing the hurt caused or harm done.

Understanding what forgiveness *is* is also very important.

- Forgiveness is required by God.
- Forgiveness is not always deserved.
- Forgiveness is impossible without God's enablement.

The mending of your emotions is a process that will take time. If you cooperate with God, His strength will enable you to forgive totally and permanently. Every time you think about an offense, you can express your feelings honestly to God and, at the same time, reaffirm your commitment to forgive. Then you can ask Him to make His love and forgiveness real to *you* so that you may view your husband with God's love and forgiveness. "Bear with each other and forgive whatever grievances you may have against one another. Forgive as the Lord forgave you" (Colossians 3:13).

Healing will require openness to God's work within you. You are facing a hard, painful process that involves a deep transformation which will start in your heart and eventually become a reality in your life. This process requires commitment and the willingness to trust in, cling to, and rely upon God as your hope and strength when you have none within yourself. In closing, I encourage you to memorize and meditate on Psalm 13:1–6, for in time, God will prove Himself faithful to you.

PART 4

Family Feuds

15

Adultery

Forgetting Is Another Story

Dear June,

My husband and I have been in intense therapy since he recently admitted to an affair of five years with the mother of our soon-to-be daughter-in-law. This person is someone I'll have to see, share grandchildren with, etc. But there is one redeeming factor in this whole mess: My husband has become a Christian. He has truly found the Lord and has a peace that I have never seen in him before. Needless to say, I'm trying to work through all my anger and bitterness. I feel I have forgiven him, but forgetting is really another story. Can you help me?

Dear Fighting-to-Forget,

Yours is truly a painfully difficult and delicate situation. Working through your hurt and reestablishing your trust will require a *process* which takes time and commitment—probably more commitment than you have ever given. In seeking God's solution on your behalf, I come back again and again to the answer that applies to any problem we have here on earth. And that is to keep your eyes on Jesus, "the author and perfecter of our faith" (Hebrews 12:2). As you look at His pattern of forgiveness I believe the following plan will be helpful.

Thank God for Your Husband's Salvation

In the midst of this painful situation, salvation is truly joyful. By focusing on this redeeming factor, continually thanking and praising God, you let the Lord soften your heart and allow Him the freedom to replace the painful memories of the past with positive memories for the future. "Be joyful always; pray continually; give thanks in all circumstances, for this is God's will for you in Christ Jesus" (1 Thessalonians 5:16–18).

Recall the Mercy God Offers You

Thank God for the grace and forgiveness He has extended to you for the wrongs you have committed in your own life. Gratefully acknowledge that He has canceled your debt and chosen not to hold any of your offenses against you or to ever bring them up again. "Bear with each other and forgive whatever grievances you may have against one another. Forgive as the Lord forgave you" (Colossians 3:13).

Face and Work Through the Past

The painful feelings about what happened must be honestly looked at and laid at the feet of Jesus. Once this is done, do not dwell on the past but put into practice Philippians 4:8.

"Finally, brethren, whatever is true, whatever is honorable, whatever is just, whatever is pure, whatever is lovely, whatever is gracious, if there is any excellence, if there is anything worthy of praise, think about these things" (RSV). Read this passage every day. Then, when a forgiven offense comes to mind, boldly think or say out loud, "I refuse to think on that! First Corinthians 13:5 says, '[Love] keeps no record of wrongs.' So I refuse to keep a ledger!"

Guard Against Any Bitterness

Hebrews 12:14,15 has a great message for you: "Make every effort to live in peace with all men and to be holy; without holiness no one will see the Lord. See to it that no one misses the grace of God and that no bitter root grows up to cause trouble and defile many." This places a great deal of responsibility on you. How you handle this trial will be the key to victory—not only for you, but for everyone.

Remember God's Character

He does all things in love.

> The LORD delights in those who fear him, who put their hope in his unfailing love (Psalm 147:11).

He always acts in fairness.

> A faithful God who does no wrong, upright and just is he (Deuteronomy 32:4).

He causes all things to work together for good.

- You intended to harm me, but God intended it for good to accomplish what is now being done (Genesis 50:20).

In choosing to forgive your husband, you have yielded to God's instruction: "Be kind and compassionate to one another, forgiving each other, just as in Christ God forgave you" (Ephesians 4:32). As you seek to live out that forgiveness in a practical way, focus on the following steps.

Forgive

F*ocus on what you can give rather than receive.*

- "It is more blessed to give than to receive" (Acts 20:35). If you are blessed, you have God's divine favor, His inner joy. You can pray, "Lord, show me what needs my husband has that I might be able to meet through Your strength."

O*vercome thoughts of the past.*

- Like Paul, practice "Forgetting what is behind and straining toward what is ahead" (Philippians 3:13) when thoughts of the emotional pain you experienced occur. Refuse to indulge this kind of thinking or else the old self-protective anger will resurface.

R*epeat Scripture in your mind.*

"Hatred stirs up dissension, but love covers over all wrongs" (Proverbs 10:12). When you are being tested, repeat relevant Bible verses or passages over and over. Remember, "Love covers, love covers, love covers." Ask God to help you to truly be a person of love—one who reflects God's love that covers over all wrongs.

***G**ive the situation to God.*

"To this you were called, because Christ suffered for you, leaving you an example, that you should follow in his steps. 'He committed no sin, and no deceit was found in his mouth.' When they hurled their insults at him, he did not retaliate; when he suffered, he made no threats. Instead, he entrusted himself to him who judges justly" (1 Peter 2:21–23). When you entrust yourself to God, you can know that every situation in your life will be used to make you better, not bitter.

***I**ntercede in behalf of your husband.*

"But I tell you: Love your enemies and pray for those who persecute you" (Matthew 5:44). "As for me, far be it from me that I should sin against the LORD by failing to pray for you" (1 Samuel 12:23). Obviously, God does not consider prayer only an option. You can pray, "Lord, glorify Yourself in my husband. Make him a man of integrity who commands the respect of all who know him. May our children and I be proud to bear his name. Manifest your character through him."

***V**erbally refuse to bring the adultery up again.*

"He who covers over an offense promotes love, but whoever repeats the matter separates close friends"

(Proverbs 17:9). After the situation has been dealt with, remember there is "a time to be silent" (Ecclesiastes 3:7). You may need to pray, "Set a guard over my mouth, O LORD; keep watch over the door of my lips" (Psalm 141:3).

***E**xpress God's grace and mercy.*

Forgiveness is an expression of God's grace and mercy toward us. Grace *is* getting what you *don't* deserve (pardon). Mercy *is not* getting what you *do* deserve (punishment). Say to God, "May my life be an expression of Your grace and Your mercy toward my husband."

As you so rightly stated in your letter, "Forgetting really is another story." The Christian life is about forgiving not forgetting. Victory comes when you *choose to remember* all the good that God accomplished through the pain. Realize you have "Christ in you" (Colossians 1:27) to forgive *through* you. His grace will enable you to forgive until the need to forgive is forgotten!

"God is able to make all grace abound to you, so that in all things at all times, having all that you need, you will abound in every good work" (2 Corinthians 9:8).

16

Career Moms

Mastering the Performance Mentality

Dear June,

I am working full-time now and fighting depression because of my deep concerns about not being the perfect mother to my three sons (ages 16, 13, and 10). My performance now cannot compare to what it used to be when I was not working. I feel too tired to really be a good homemaker. My husband and boys pitch in at home and want me to continue to work, but my convictions leave me with great feelings of being out of God's will. I feel that I am not blessed and joyful like I used to be because of my priorities. Please help!

Dear Tired Performer,

Many sincere people share your deep concern about being the "perfect parent." My heart especially hurts for working mothers juggling the demanding responsibilities of both family and career. While your high standards of parenting are admirable, you have reached the end of your own resources with your relentless push to perform and "keep all the balls in the air." Take heart! You are now at the place where you may be willing to receive some of God's precious truths that can relieve your pressure, restore your peace, and reorder your priorities.

Praise God for the privilege of parenting!

In the pressure of daily routine it is easy to forget that rearing children, while a difficult challenge for a time, is still a gift from the Lord. Psalm 127:3 says, "Sons are a heritage from the LORD, children a reward from him." God gave you these unique sons, and their time with you is short compared to the rest of their lives. What a joyous opportunity is yours to plant seeds of godly character and watch them grow in the lives of your boys as they mature into godly young men!

Accept your present limitations.

How tempting it must be to remember the days when you enjoyed being a full-time homemaker. However, with a full-time working schedule you are now limited in both time and energy. Comparing your present situation with your past parenting performance will reap only regret and drain you of the desire to do what you can. Remember—God knows your limitations, yet He still allows these boys to be in your care.

Teach your sons how to do more household chores to contribute to the family. The more proficient they become at taking care of themselves and the home, the more competent they will feel and the better prepared they will be for living independently as young adults. If your pattern has been to do everything for them, you may have unknowingly set the stage for them to be more dependent than is needful. God is the God of your circumstances, and you can trust Him to use the present situation to better equip your boys for the future He has in store for them.

Talk to God and tell Him, "Thank you, Lord, for how You will use my working outside the home in the lives of each of my family members." We are to "give thanks in all circumstances, for this is God's will for you in Christ Jesus" (1 Thessalonians 5:18).

***R**ealize your precious value in Christ's family.*

How important for you to understand that your personal value is rooted in who you *are,* not in what you *do.* (That's why we are called human *be*-ings, not human *do*-ings!) Your performance as a parent neither adds to nor subtracts from God's acceptance of you. God sees you as His valued child—*unconditionally* accepted, forgiven, and loved. As you read Romans 8:31–39, tuck inside your heart the last verse, "Neither height nor depth, nor anything else in all creation, will be able to separate [me] from the love of God that is in Christ Jesus our Lord."

***E**xpand your ministry to the workplace.*

What was God's purpose for leading you into a career and placing you where you are? Through your influence, perhaps a coworker will enter into an authentic relationship with the Lord Jesus Christ. Or you may be able to encourage others by the joyful manner in which you approach your work. Thank the Lord for your job and begin to pray specifically for your coworkers. Focusing on the needs of others will help you gain a positive perspective—"And whatever you do, whether in word or deed, do it all in the name of the Lord Jesus, giving thanks to God the Father through him. . . . Whatever you do, work at it with all your heart, as working for the Lord, not for men" (Colossians 3:17,23).

***N**ote any negativity*

The enemy of your soul wants to use flaming darts of *discouragement* to oppress you. Don't dwell on your disappointments or depressing thoughts. Claim the comfort of His promises (such as Hebrews 13:5: "I will never leave you or forsake you"). When negative feelings of self-doubt well up within you, obey the positive words of Philippians 4:8: "Whatever is true, whatever is noble, whatever is right, whatever is pure, whatever is lovely, whatever is admirable—if anything is excellent or praiseworthy—think about such things." Poring over God's promises and resting in God's sovereignty will shift your focus from "self" to the Savior.

***T**ake control of your time.*

Begin to cherish time as a treasured gift from God, then use it wisely by investing in that which will have eternal results. Ephesians 5:15,16 warns us to "be very careful, then, how you live—not as unwise but as wise, making the most of every opportunity, because the days are evil."

- *Prioritize* your activities according to what has more long-term benefit. Is it more important to clean a kitchen immediately after dinner or to spend quality time with one of your children? "Therefore do not be foolish, but understand what the Lord's will is" (Ephesians 5:17).

- *Pray* for God to give you discernment between that which is good and that which would be better. " 'Everything is permissible for me'—but not everything is beneficial" (1 Corinthians 6:12).

- *Plan* ahead and follow through on specific goals for spending time with your children. Family Fun Nights are effective in building close-knit families. For example, plan a regular bowling or miniature golf night or game nights at home—with popcorn, of course. Schedule a fascinating family vacation. Seek out one-on-one quality time with each son each week. Don't let outside pressures deter the accomplishment of your goals. "An upright man [and mom!] gives thought to his [and her] ways" (Proverbs 21:29).

- *Practice* how to say, *No!* It is not unspiritual to say *no.* Because many people will pressure you and plead for your time and attention, it is easy to become encumbered with that which keeps you from what is most important. Periodically evaluate:

> "Am I now trying to win the approval of men, or of God? Or am I trying to please men? If I were still trying to please men, I would not be a servant of Christ" (Galatians 1:10).

The first letter in each of these six main points spell the word PARENT . . . the most important job title you will ever have! God calls you to reflect the character of Christ before your boys and He will equip you to do it!

But thanks be to God! He gives us the victory through our Lord Jesus Christ (1 Corinthians 15:57).

17

Dysfunctional Families

PEACE WITH YOUR PAST

Dear June,

I was brought up in a family where both parents were workaholics and one was an alcoholic. They refused to accept their responsibilities as parents, so I became the parent and they became the children. Even though I am now an adult living on my own, they're still doing the same things as before. I feel guilty for moving out even though an older brother still lives at home. Do you have any advice that could help me?

Dear Role-Reverser,

Typically, the pain and frustrating patterns of living in a dysfunctional family flow well into adulthood. The improper behavior of even one parent can damage individuality and sabotage relational skills among all family members. But take heart—there *is* hope! Though you can never change the past, you *can* change your attitude about the past. You can also learn new ways to *respond* to your parents rather than *react* to their behavior.

Reconcile the Past

To live life now with more joy and to have a more hopeful future, release the pain of your past. We often fail to perceive that God uses our pain for our benefit. For example, in the Bible, Joseph's family was very dysfunctional (lack of communication, favoritism, jealousy, dishonesty, anger, revenge, disloyalty, fear), but Joseph broke free from his family's character flaws. He cultivated a strong spiritual walk by yielding to God's ways. He was not a prisoner of his past. In fact, he said to his brothers, "You intended to harm me, but God intended it for good" (Genesis 50:20). Like Joseph, you too can deal with your past and be stronger for it. The choice to change is yours!

- *Allow yourself time to grieve.* Ecclesiastes 3:4 says there is "a time to weep and a time to laugh, a time to mourn and a time to dance." You might ask a wise friend to help you talk through your past hurts, starting from your early years and continuing to the present. Pray for God to reveal all your repressed pain. When He does, be honest about your anger and give yourself permission to grieve.
- *Choose to have a heart of forgiveness.* Colossians 3:13 reminds us that God calls us to forgive those who have hurt us, just as He forgives us when we hurt Him. It is helpful to consider the consequences of unforgiveness—specifically, a critical and bitter

spirit. Since *forgiveness is a process,* you must continually forgive, again and again, and quickly make the choice to release your hurt to the Lord.

- *Give thanks for your past.* First Thessalonians 5:18 tells us to be thankful in all circumstances. Even though you don't feel thankful, you can choose to acknowledge that God uses difficult relationships to bring you to maturity. Look at the positive way God has used this situation to give you compassion for other people. Focus on what you can be thankful for.

Respond to the Present

The past is the past, but each moment is a new opportunity to respond positively to the present. This can be referred to as the "precious present," because each moment offers an opportunity to be aware of the presence of God and offers an opportunity to submit your will to Christ, allowing Him to be Lord of all you think and do. Here are three ways to evaluate and modify your responses.

- *Take a look at your own dysfunctions.* Psalm 22:23,24 says, "You who fear the LORD, praise him! . . . For he has not despised or disdained the suffering of the afflicted one; he has not hidden his face from him but has listened to his cry for help." Pray for the Lord to reveal ways you responded to your parents as a child and what patterns you are still following. Are you trying to get your needs met by being super-responsible or by fixing family problems? Do you feel valuable only when you are in control?

Pray for wisdom to discern your distorted thinking patterns.

- *Allow the Lord to be your Need-Meeter.* You were created with the God-given inner needs for love, significance and security. The Lord designed you that way so that you would *rely on Him* to meet your deepest needs. Philippians 4:19 states, "My God will meet all your needs . . ." The more dependent you are on the Lord, the less dependent you will be on your parents. For example, you have done much for your parents which has made you feel significant . . . temporarily. But when you need time for yourself (even as Jesus did), you feel guilty. If you allow the Lord to be your Need-Meeter, He will affirm that you are *already* significant—not because of what you do, but because of what He has done for you. He created you and He died for you! Thank you Jesus.

- *Establish boundaries.* Acts 5:29 says "We must obey God rather than men." You have the right to obey God rather than people, the right to a clear conscience, and the right to be led by the Word of God. Decide now that you will no longer be manipulated by being guilt-jerked. Let your parents take responsibility for their own lives.

As an adult you are no longer powerless; so you don't need to react like a victim. Instead, take responsibility for your own behavior. It is important to learn *when* and *how* to say no. When you are being pressured to do something but don't feel led by the Spirit of God, say no. If you are being manipulated to change your commitments or violate your conscience, say no. Memorize Galatians 1:10 and repeat it to yourself when you are being "people-pressured" instead of being "Spirit-led": "Am I now trying to win the approval of men, or of God? Or am I trying to please men? If I were still trying to please men, I would not be a servant of Christ."

- *Speak the truth in love.* Proverbs 16:21 says, "The wise in heart are called discerning, and pleasant words promote instruction." Without laying blame tell your parents that you need to have some changes in your own life. Perhaps say, "I haven't always responded to you in the healthiest way. Please forgive me. Sometimes I've blamed you for making me feel guilty, when in reality I had false guilt. If I'm not guilty, it's my responsibility not to *feel* guilty. . . . I want to be able to give to you out of love, not guilt.

  "At times, you might want me to do one thing, but if I feel I need to do something else, I hope you will understand. Even if you don't understand, I still need to do what I think is best. It is not healthy for me to go against my conscience. . . . Can we agree to be open and honest about our desires and to respect each other's decisions? Let's give each other freedom and have the best relationship possible."

- *Give up your need to control.* In Luke 9:23 Jesus says, "If anyone would come after me, he must deny himself and take up his cross daily and follw me."

This means that instead of you being in control, you give Christ control. Let the Lord *be lord* of your life. If you have humbled your heart and asked Christ to come into your life, then you have "Christ in you" (Colossians 1:27) to be the power source for you. With His constant presence and through His power, you can experience positive change.

Rebuild for the Future

Your own relationships can be healthy and enjoyable. Remember that in a healthy family, parental structure is maintained, individuality is encouraged, positive relationships are developed, and problems are confronted. Though all of this takes time and continuous effort, be encouraged "for it is God who works in you to will and to act according to his good purpose" (Philippians 2:13).

As you tear down your past negative responses to being manipulated and start building new, healthy, nonmanipulated patterns, anticipate resistance and pain from your parents. Change is always hard and painful. But this is necessary pain—pain with a purpose. Cling to the Lord Jesus Christ, cast your cares on Him, and claim the unconditional love God has for you.

18

Mid-Life Crisis

Roller Coaster Runaway

Dear June,

My husband of twenty-nine years is going through a mid-life crisis, but he will not admit this is his problem. Our children (17 and 22) and I were shocked to find his letter saying that he was leaving. He says he sees our marriage as the main problem, but at the same time he refuses the counseling that could heal it.

In my heart I feel that my husband is feeling very bad about himself and has given up. I think he is afraid of real closeness and has just run away from everything and everybody, including God and the church. Our entire family is devastated because he has always been a strong and godly leader. What can I do to help myself and our children get through this? What can I do to help him? I feel so out of control.

Dear Out of Control,

I hear the desperation in your heart as you describe your husband's runaway actions. The breakdown of a marriage is emotionally terrifying. It's like riding a runaway roller coaster all alone, with no one to cling to, and you don't know where or how to get off. Your only choice seems to be hanging on and enduring the ride. But for God's children it doesn't have to be like that. We do have someone to cling to . . . a companion who will ride with us all the way.

During this time of immense grief and uncertainty, I pray that you will rely on God's faithfulness toward you! Take comfort from His words in Psalms by reading four chapters a night before you go to sleep. Rely on His presence and count on His promise that He is close to the brokenhearted and will deliver you from all your fears.

> The righteous cry out, and the LORD hears them; he delivers them from all their troubles. The LORD is close to the brokenhearted and saves those who are crushed in spirit (Psalm 34:17,18).

One of the hardest obstacles to overcome will be the tendency to take your husband's behavior personally. The sense of rejection you feel can be overwhelming, but your husband's mid-life crisis is more *his personal spiritual problem* than it is a marital problem. All marriages have difficulties, but if one partner hardens his or her heart toward the other, that spouse is acting like a rebellious child, running from the sovereign claim God has on each of our lives. And yes, you will suffer the consequences of your husband's behavior, but in reality his consequences will be more far-reaching.

> "Woe to the obstinate children," declares the LORD, "to those who carry out plans that are not mine, forming an alliance, but not by my Spirit, heaping sin upon sin" (Isaiah 30:1).

Maybe it will help you to become more objective and even to have a heart of compassion for your husband if you can understand some of the feelings and emotions he is experiencing. Many people during their later years in life (35–60) go through transitional times when they feel the necessity to reevaluate their identity, their values, and their goals. Often, when the roller coaster of life begins to accelerate, people who fear aging begin to experience feelings of loss, self-pity, and doubt. These feelings create a sense of doom if they stay on their present track. The crucial point comes when they determine that change must occur. This *change* can mean a deeper spiritual growth in the Lord or it can mean the sometimes selfish pursuit of a different ride. The following thoughts and events can trigger fear in the heart of one who is in mid-life:

- Dread of one's own mortality
- Reassessment of lifelong goals and values
- Achievement of goals but not finding fulfillment
- Insufficient financial resources
- Traumatic illness or death in the family
- Children at a difficult age or leaving home
- Dissatisfaction with chosen career
- Loss of sexual drive

If these fears are allowed to take hold in the thought process, the one seeking change begins to rationalize and decide, "I am trapped in a life that is unfulfilling. I deserve a chance to make changes before it is too late to discover my own identity and find personal happiness." But God says, "Do you see a man wise in his own eyes? There is more hope for a fool than for him" (Proverbs 26:12).

You mentioned in your letter that you feel your husband "is feeling very bad about himself." You are probably right! I realize you want to help him, but at this point your words will have little effect. Your anxiety will lessen if you take your eyes off your husband's problem and begin to focus on your own inner attitudes. Develop attitudes that communicate respect and concern for him.

> Wives, in the same way be submissive to your husbands so that, if any of them do not believe the word, they may be won over without words by the behavior of their wives (1 Peter 3:1).

What You Can *Do*

- Pray daily for your husband. This will protect you from getting a hardened heart.
- Get spiritual strength from reading God's Word daily and being with God's people often.
- Let go of any expectations that your husband will show appreciation or affection toward you.
- Understand the emotional battle your husband is experiencing: failure, fear, frustration.
- Be prepared for his anger to be directed toward you, but don't answer his anger with anger.
- Find ways to gently encourage him to discuss his feelings . . . talk on a feeling level.
- Read and learn as much as you can about mid-life crisis.

- Encourage him to talk to a Christ-centered counselor with you or to speak to an informed spiritual leader who understands mid-life crisis.
- Ask those closest to him to "speak the truth in love". . . if they are led to by the Lord.
- Refuse to nag or pressure him. Instead, reaffirm his God-given worth.
- Maintain an attractive appearance—don't become unkempt.
- Develop a gentle, quiet spirit toward your husband and the present circumstances surrounding your family.

> [Your beauty] should be that of your inner self, the unfading beauty of a gentle and quiet spirit, which is of great worth in God's sight (1 Peter 3:4).

In closing, let me emphasize that you and your children will be safe for the ride. God knows what is happening to your family. *He is in control!* He alone can fight your fears, provide your peace, and meet all the emotional and physical needs you will ever have. He is the *only* one you can count on to get through all the ups and downs in life.

> *The Lord himself goes before you and will be with you; he will never leave you nor forsake you. Do not be afraid; do not be discouraged* (Deuteronomy 31:8).

19

Parenting

Eight Going on Twelve

Dear June,

I feel I've blown it as a mother. My eight-year-old thinks she's a twelve-year-old and has developed a fresh mouth, talking in a very disrespectful way to me. I explained to her that talking to me in this manner is wrong and really hurts me, but this hasn't helped. I feel if I don't do something, I'll only have more problems with her later. What would you suggest?

Dear Tired Mother,

Parenting is a demanding and often tough job that carries responsibilities which can seem especially enormous in difficult circumstances . . . but it's wonderful to know you have a loving God who desires to give you guidance and has your daughter's best interest at heart.

You are wise in seeking to deal with your daughter's disrespectful behavior now because behavior which goes unchecked will not only continue but will likely worsen. As you explore ways in which you might address this problem with your daughter, I encourage you to first examine some biblical principles regarding discipline. Before you determine *what* to do, it is important to be confident about your *why* in doing it. Also, if you are not absolutely certain about the goal behind your need to take action, you will find it too easy to let inappropriate behaviors slide. The strength and motivation to discipline is often found in the goal ahead and the "why" behind it.

The Whys of Discipline

God sheds light on the "why" behind discipline in Proverbs 13:24, "He who spares the rod hates his son, but he who loves him is careful to discipline him." According to this passage, conscientious parents who provide positive structure and protective limits do so out of love. Giving love means setting limits. You cannot love without setting limits, but you can set limits without love. The key to setting *effective* limits is setting them *in love.*

The Goals of Discipline

First Timothy 3:4 spotlights one of the goals of discipline: "He must manage his own family well and see that his children obey him with proper respect." In this Scripture God expresses His command that your daughter be taught obedience and respect *by* and *for* you. If your daughter learns to obey and respect people in authority, she will be more willing to obey and respect the one who establishes authority—*God!* It will be easier for her to obey Him, whom she cannot see or hear with physical eyes and ears, after she has learned to obey you, whom she can see and hear.

Another goal is found in Ephesians 6:4: "Bring them up in the training and instruction of the Lord." Of course your ultimate goal in parenting is to lead your daughter into a personal awareness of her need of a savior and into a personal relationship with *the* Savior, the Lord Jesus Christ. By training and instructing her through words and deeds, then living out the character of Christ before her, you are doing your part in laying a foundation which is most likely to ensure that she will ultimately choose Christ. To your daughter you are an earthly reflection of the unseen God. By His design, you are God's instrument for meeting your daughter's needs in a way that will awaken her spiritual sensitivity and draw her to the Lord.

A third goal for discipline which speaks directly to your situation is stated in Proverbs 29:15, "The rod of correction imparts *wisdom,* but a child left to himself disgraces his mother." According to this Scripture, your daughter's disgraceful behavior is symptomatic of the fact that she is lacking in wisdom. And, as you stated in your letter, the disgraceful behavior will certainly continue unless you intervene. Her *need* is for wisdom, and the *way* you impart that wisdom to her is through the *rod of correction.*

The Don'ts of Discipline

> He who spares the rod hates his son, but he who loves him is careful to discipline him (Proverbs 13:24).

Don't feel guilty when you discipline your child. You are loving your child when you hold the line on limits.

Don't be afraid of losing your child's love. By doing God's will you will earn your child's respect.

Don't view structure and limits as punishment. You are establishing beneficial boundaries.

Don't try to manipulate your child with fear or guilt. See discipline as positive correction to put your child back on a correct course.

Don't embarrass your child in front of others. Praise in public and correct in private.

Don't belittle your child with sarcasm. Speak the truth in love and correct with compassion.

Don't compare your child with others. See your child as a unique creation of God.

Don't discipline your child in anger. Wait for your anger to pass as you pray for wisdom to discipline appropriately.

Don't use your hand for correction. Use a neutral object—not a father's belt or a mother's brush—but an object, such as a paddle.

The Do's of Discipline

> The rod of correction imparts wisdom, but a child left to himself disgraces his mother (Proverbs 29:15).

Do mold the will without breaking the spirit. (Colossians 3:21).

- A child's will is molded by applying appropriate discipline when the child seeks to go in a direction contrary to the will of the parents.
- A child's spirit is uplifted by being valued as a unique creation of God and by being treated with kindness and respect.
- A child's spirit can be broken in an atmosphere of overreacting to too many rules, criticizing or teasing, false accusations or inflexibility, impatience or harsh punishment.

Do communicate your expectations early (Revelation 3:19).

- Get on your child's eye level.
- Prior to any problems, describe in detail what you expect of your child regarding structure and limits.
- Get an agreement and ask your child to repeat his or her understanding of your expectations.
- When it is time for your child to obey, give one gentle reminder. Don't say: "Don't you think it's time for you to go to bed now?" Do say: "Remember, we agreed that your bedtime is 9:00. It's 8:40 now, so what do you need to be doing?"

Do establish negative consequences for misbehavior (Proverbs 19:18).

- To establish effective consequences, know your child's likes and dislikes.
- Choose a consequence related to the behavior.
- Clearly communicate the consequence.

- Prior to the problem, get your child's agreement to the consequence.
- Allow your child to experience the consequence for disobedience.

Do use spanking when a child defies your authority (Proverbs 23:13).

- Spanking is primarily for toddlers and preschoolers (not infants and teenagers).
- Spank your child in private.
- Never spank your child in anger, but rather in sorrow.
- Explain the reason for the spanking.
- Ask your child to repeat the reason why the spanking is being given.
- Give a few swift, painful swats on the buttocks.
- Verbally and physically comfort your child immediately after the spanking.
- Spanking should be used only when productive. (Some children don't require spanking for repentance; others don't respond to spanking.)

Do encourage and develop responsibility (Proverbs 17:25).

- Allow your child to make choices and decisions.
- Permit your child to experience the consequences of wrong choices and the benefits of right choices.
- Give increased freedom when your child is responsible.

- Restrict freedom when your child is irresponsible. "You may not play on the yard any more today, but we will try it again tomorrow."

Do assign beneficial chores (Proverbs 14:23).

- Chores need to be assigned to everyone in the family.
- Chores need to be explained as benefiting the whole family.
- Chores need to be clearly detailed.
- Chores need to be compatible with your child's capabilities.
- Chores need to be given an assigned time for completion.
- Chores need to be consistently enforced by making sure they are done.

Do reinforce positive behavior (Hebrews 10:25b).

- Give your child praise regarding character traits. "Your room looks great. I'm proud of your faithfulness to finish the job well."
- Give your child "thank yous." "I really appreciate your willingness to help bring in the groceries. Thanks for your help."
- Give your child recognition in front of others. "Jim, I wish you had heard the compliments on the way our lawn looked after Susan picked up the trash on it."
- Give your child attention. "Susan, I heard you have learned to dive from the side of the pool. I would love to see you dive."

- Give your child respect. "Susan, I respect your need for privacy. I won't enter your room without knocking."
- Give your child smiles and physical affection. Children need to be lovingly touched by their parents—with plenty of hugs, kisses, squeezes, pats on the back or a hand on the shoulder.

Do maintain consistency (Proverbs 24:3,4).

- Both parents need to come to agreement in private on issues regarding the children, even if they disagree.
- Make only promises you can keep.
- Give careful thought to a request before denying it.
- Refrain from requiring too many major changes at one time.
- Evaluate your rules, and change them as your child grows.

Consistency is one of the most important habits a parent needs to develop. If you take the time to give careful thought over each decision before making it, you stand a better chance of avoiding making promises you can't deliver. Remember that children are only temporary gifts from God. As a bow is made to propel the arrow toward the target, you are there to enable your daughter or son to soar toward God's goal . . . helping your child conform to the character of Christ.

PART
5

Anchored Alone

20

Childlessness

A Time for Trust

Dear June,

My husband and I have been struggling with infertility for years. We have been praying for a baby. I have cried out to the Lord for so long now. Furthermore, the emotional stress and strain this has placed upon us and our marriage is almost indescribable. What I need to know is: Does the Lord want us to have a baby? If so, when? Since God promises to bless the parents whose "quiver is full" of children, why has God withheld children from us?

Dear Empty Quiver,

How I wish I could answer confidently, "Yes! Yes, your baby is due in eight-and-a-half months!" But no one on earth knows the future. That's why those who are wise learn to walk by faith, not by sight.

Although you don't know the future, you do know *who* holds the future. But do you really trust God with *your* future? Let me assure you, the more intimately you know Him, the more thoroughly you will trust Him. Take comfort in what the prophet Isaiah said long ago:

> The LORD longs to be gracious to you; he rises to show you compassion. For the LORD is a God of justice. Blessed are all who wait for him! . . . Whether you turn to the right or to the left, your ears will hear a voice behind you, saying, "This is the way; walk in it" (Isaiah 30:18,21).

Ultimately, when you know the core of God's character, you can trust Him with what you don't have as well as with what you do have.

Trust God with What You Don't Have

Don't be consumed with what you don't have,
  for your childless life is not "less."
Trust the Lord with His perfect plan,
  then your child-free life He will bless.

Trust Him with the Whys

There is nothing wrong in asking, *Why?* But don't demand the answer now. In time you will see and understand. Deuteronomy 32:4 says of the Lord, "All his ways are just. A faithful God who does no wrong, upright and just is he." In time you will see how—in His justice—He strengthened you with insights you would not have seen otherwise. Through this time of intense struggle, you can trust Him to work in you and through you to do what is best for you.

Until you have "eyes to see" His purpose, hang onto this promise: "And we know that in all things God works for the good of those who love him, who have been called according to his purpose" (Romans 8:28).

Trust Him with Your Future

Not only is God with you but He is also a provider for you. Even now, He has a plan and a purpose for your life. He says: "For I know the plans I have for you . . . plans to prosper you and not to harm you, plans to give you hope and a future" (Jeremiah 29:11). Instead of viewing your life as child-less, see yourself as child-free. Don't focus on the disadvantages. Instead, focus on all the available advantages (more time for spiritual growth, special projects, close friendships, more schooling, discipling others, hobbies and crafts, travel, and such). Begin to open your heart to a child-free marriage as you claim 1 Timothy 6:6: "Godliness with contentment is great gain."

During this time, when it's hard to see what the future may hold, write the following Scriptures on cards and read them three times each day, aloud if possible:

> Trust in the LORD with all your heart and lean not on your own understanding; in all your ways acknowledge him, and he will make your paths straight (Proverbs 3:5,6).
>
> In his heart a man plans his course, but the LORD determines his steps (Proverbs 16:9).
>
> The LORD is close to the brokenhearted and saves those who are crushed in spirit (Psalm 34:18).

> I will instruct you and teach you in the way you should go; I will counsel you and watch over you (Psalm 32:8).
>
> I am still confident of this: I will see the goodness of the LORD in the land of the living. Wait for the LORD; be strong and take heart and wait for the LORD (Psalm 27:13,14).
>
> My comfort in my suffering is this: Your promise preserves my life (Psalm 119:50).

Trust God with What You Do Have

Don't assume that childlessness is less. Thank God daily for His promises and for what He is providing. Take time to value your husband, your health, your family and friends, your salvation, and your Savior. If you cultivate a heart of thanksgiving you will change your focus from what you *don't* have to what you *do* have. You will also find that *sowing seeds of gratitude will greatly change your attitude.* A positive outlook of anticipation will fill your future with hope and healing. What can you anticipate? Consider and claim God's promise:

> Forget the former things; do not dwell on the past. See, I am doing a new thing! Now it springs up; do you not perceive it? I am making a way in the desert and streams in the wasteland (Isaiah 43:18,19).

Possibilities for a Deeper and More Fulfilling Marriage

Realize that during this time of crisis you and your husband can drive each other away or draw each other closer—it all depends on the quality of your commitment. Now is the time to:

- Cultivate a deep bond in your relationship (Genesis 2:24).
- Communicate daily the love you have for each other (Ephesians 5:22–28).
- Confess your feelings and fears of not having children (Proverbs 24:26).
- Confront the difficulties and differences directly (Proverbs 27:5).
- Compliment, affirm, and support each other verbally (Ephesians 4:29).

If you have not already done so, call a "team" meeting—sit down with your husband and discuss your desires and lay out all your options. Share how you as a couple could invest your time together during this waiting period. Your options are numerous. I especially encourage you to spend time nurturing and encouraging others.

Possibilities for Birth Children

You may feel as if you are walking alone, but you are by no means by yourself—one in six married couples find themselves infertile. Even more common is secondary infertility (the inability to give birth following one successful pregnancy). Don't assume that all infertile couples are sterile. While sterility is an irreversible condition, infertility is a current condition that possibly can be altered. (For example, certain medications can cause infertility, as can a below-normal body weight.)

Since many infertile couples stay frustrated, not knowing that help could be around the corner, consider the best beginning steps for you and your husband:

- Get a thorough medical checkup.
- Consult an infertility specialist.
- Get a second opinion if your doctor is not responsive.
- Read books and articles on infertility.
- Talk with others who have walked down a similar path.

> Plans fail for lack of counsel, but with many advisers they succeed (Proverbs 15:22).

Possibilities for Adopting Children

Have you considered adoption as a serious option? Don't presume that this route is a detour from God's best. Not only was baby Moses adopted only to become the leader of his land, but you too were adopted by God according to His plan. Adoption was God's chosen route for making you His child, for "He predestined us to be adopted as his sons through Jesus Christ, in accordance with his pleasure and will" (Ephesians 1:5). Adoption is a picture of the Lord's perfect love. Just realize: He didn't have to adopt you . . . He *chose* you to be His child!

Ask the Lord if He is opening your heart to the option of adoption. Talk with your husband about his desires and answer these questions honestly:

- Could you take an infant, a baby who needs a home, into your hearts?
- Could you adopt an older child—perhaps from a foster home?
- Could you handle a hard-to-place child who has special needs?
- Could you choose a child of a different race or heritage?
- Could you open your home to a young child from a foreign land?

Don't forget: "God sets the lonely in families" (Psalm 68:6).

If you both are so led—and you must be led—then open your hearts' door to adoption. If it is His will, He will lead you through the door every step of the way. Then these thoughts can be your prayer:

> Lord, although adoption was my second choice, I see it is not "second best." Just as by adoption You have made me feel secure in Your family, I am willing for a child of Your choosing to feel secure in our family.

Possibilities for Spiritual Children

Look for opportunities to love and nurture others. Because of the perspective you are learning through pain, God is preparing you to have a ministry in the lives of others.

The Lord will pour compassion into you, for you to pour into others.

> [He is] the Father of compassion and the God of all comfort, who comforts us in all our troubles, so that we can comfort those in any trouble with the comfort we ourselves have received from God (2 Corinthians 1:3,4).

I assure you, if your focus is on the needs of others, especially young people, you will find your "quiver" delightfully full of sons and daughters in the faith. You, too, will see that this Scripture applies to you: "Blessed is the man whose quiver is full of them" (Psalm 127:5).

So, how do you make yourself ready for this ministry?

- *Pray for God to prepare the hearts of those who really need you.* Keep on the outlook for those He will send your way (see Galatians 6:2).
- *Invest yourself in the lives of extended family members.* Prioritize one-on-one "talk times" with nieces, nephews, and younger cousins (see Proverbs 16:23).
- *Prepare yourself to answer the challenging questions of the faith.* Read books on apologetics and give them as gifts (see 1 Peter 3:15).
- *Ask the Lord to initiate each relationship and activity.* Be open to teaching Sunday school, tutoring a teen, providing training in a skill (see Proverbs 16:9).

- *Decide to be a discipler in the areas where God has taught you.* Ask God to give you a disciple who is hungry for spiritual growth (see Matthew 28:19,20).

Though you are physically childless, your "spiritual children" can be more meaningful and numerous than you could ever imagine. Don't hold back; reach beyond the normal bounds and gather them in with the guidance of God.

> *"Sing, O barren woman, you who never bore a child; burst into song, shout for joy, you who were never in labor; because more are the children of the desolate woman than of her who has a husband," says the* LORD. *"Enlarge the place of your tent, stretch your tent curtains wide, do not hold back; lengthen your cords, strengthen your stakes"* (Isaiah 54:1,2).

21

Divorce

New Beginnings

Dear June,

For the past three years, I have been going through severe emotional, physical, and financial problems. My husband left my ten-year-old son and me for another woman. Our son is not adjusting very well and his father will have nothing to do with him.

My ex-husband and his new wife are prospering (new house, new car, etc.) while my son and I are in financial poverty. He will not help us financially at all. I am unable to keep a job for any length of time due to health problems. I used to be a very pretty young woman, but now I feel ugly and I don't understand why things have happened the way they have.

I am crying as I write to you. My son and I desperately need someone to care for us and lift us out of this depression. I am so lonely and depressed that sometimes I don't even want to go on anymore.

Dear Starting Over,

The breakup of a marriage is an emotionally devastating experience. I heard a broken heart crying out from each line of your letter. During this most difficult time of grief and adjustment, I pray you will learn to rely on God's faithfulness to you and realize how special you are as His child. He is the one who longs to *care for* you and your son. He is the one who can *lift you out of the depression* with His arms of love. God alone knows how to heal your hurts and transform your pain into joy. "Heal me, O LORD, and I will be healed; save me and I will be saved, for you are the one I praise" (Jeremiah 17:14). Especially now, since your husband has remarried, you will have to accept the reality that it is time for you to embark on a new beginning. And since God is patiently waiting for you to give Him a chance, allow Him to work a miraculous new change in your life.

Change Your Thinking

See yourself as God sees you.

You have great worth and value to God. Take heart, for the Lord says, "You are precious and honored in my sight . . . I love you" (Isaiah 43:4). Whenever you have demeaning thoughts about yourself, read Psalm 139:1–16.

Sense God's presence with you.

God has promised never to leave you, "For the LORD your God goes with you; he will never leave you nor forsake you" (Deuteronomy 31:6). Another promise of His abiding presence is in Psalm 34:18, "The LORD is close to the brokenhearted and saves those who are crushed in spirit."

Seek God's purpose for you.

Do you realize God planned a specific purpose for you before you were born? Memorize Jeremiah 29:11: " 'For I know the plans I have for you,' declares the LORD, 'plans to prosper you and not to harm you, plans to give you hope and a future.' " What is happening to you now has not caught Him by surprise. He is aware of your situation and His plans cannot be thwarted.

Stop all disastrous comparisons.

Even though it requires self-discipline, you must make every effort to take your eyes off your former husband and his appearance of prosperity. Realize that Satan (your adversary) will try to convince you that everything is wonderful in that household and that there is something wrong with you and your son. This is simply not true! If you spend time with the truth of Psalm 37, you will see why you need to bypass this pitfall of comparison.

Surrender your fears about your finances.

When Paul told the Philippians, "My God will meet all your needs according to his glorious riches in Christ Jesus" (Philippians 4:19), he was referring specifically to their financial needs. Can you release expectations that your former husband will take care of you? Can you trust God to provide for your financial needs if you fulfill your responsibilities and honor Him with the resources you do have?

Steer your son toward God.

Turn your son's heart toward the Lord. Help him feel secure in the safety of the love and protection of his heavenly Father: "A father to the fatherless, a defender of widows, is God in his holy dwelling" (Psalm 68:5). Above all, purpose not to express negative attitudes toward your former husband in the presence of your son.

Search for inner healing.

Realize that you cannot change anyone else, but God can change you. He will heal areas within you that need His touch. Pray Psalm 139:23,24: "Search me, O God, and know my heart; test me and know my anxious thoughts. See if there is any offensive way in me, and lead me in the way everlasting." Once God brings to your mind inappropriate thoughts and attitudes, write them down and commit each one of them to the Lord. Then seek practical ways of working with God to make changes in those areas. Should He reveal ways in which you have wrongfully pained others, confess to God and to them and then claim God's forgiveness and seek their forgiveness.

Change Your Dependency

God created you to need love (unconditional love and acceptance), significance (meaning and purpose in life), and a sense of security. *These needs are designed to draw you to God*—the only one who can meet them perfectly. Although He often works through people to meet some of these needs, hurt and disillusionment result when *you* place your expectations in someone other than God.

The Christian life is a relationship with the person of Jesus Christ, whose Spirit lives within you and desires to express Himself through you. You will experience joy, freedom, and fulfillment as you choose to live minute-by-minute, hour-by-hour, day-by-day *in dependence on Him.* He is your strength, your power, and your hope. To help exchange your weakness for God's strength, claim Philippians 4:13: "I have strength for all things in Christ Who empowers me [I am ready for anything and equal to anything through Him Who infuses inner strength into me; I am self-sufficient in Christ's sufficiency]" (AMP).

Your responsibility is to submit yourself to God and allow Him to transform you and to manifest His life within you from the inside out. Romans 12:1 says, "Therefore, I urge you, brothers, in view of God's mercy, to offer your bodies as living sacrifices, holy and pleasing to God—this is your spiritual act of worship."

Change Your Feelings

Face your feelings. Deal with your feelings honestly. Don't try to ignore or deny them. Bring your tears, hurt, confusion, anger, fear, and frustration to Jesus who died for the right to bear your pain. Run to Him as a hurt and crying child, pour out your heart to Him and receive His comfort. Remember that "we do not have a high priest who is unable to sympathize with our weaknesses, but we have one who has been tempted in every way, just as we are—yet was without sin. Let us then approach the throne of grace with confidence, so that we may receive mercy and find grace to help us in our time of need" (Hebrews 4:15,16).

Face forgiveness. Even in the midst of the pain of your wounded heart, God calls you to forgive your former husband. *Forgiveness is decided in the mind.* It is an *act of the will* and can be extended *regardless of how you feel.* It does not keep the forgiven person from facing the just consequences of his sin before God, but it keeps you from becoming embittered, which is the consequence of failing to forgive. (Read Hebrews 12:14,15.)

Face your singleness. Accept your singleness as the place God wants you to be right now. "Give thanks in all circumstances, for this is God's will for you in Christ Jesus" (1 Thessalonians 5:18). Are you involved in a local church? You and your son will greatly benefit by getting involved with other people. How helpful it would be if you could find a mature, godly woman who would encourage you for a period of time. Surround yourself with and invest yourself in people who can be emotionally and spiritually supportive.

Although it is hard, try not to allow yourself to become discouraged or to give up. Remember, your son is sensing your feelings of discouragement and applying them to himself. Let him see the power of God working in your life as you embark on new beginnings.

Change Your Identity

Remember:

- Your new identity is in the Lord, not in a position or another person (read Galatians 2:20).
- You are complete in Christ, not incomplete as a single person (read Colossians 2:9,10).

- Your happiness comes from inner attitudes, not outer circumstances (read Matthew 5:3–12).
- Your purpose in life is to glorify God (read 1 Corinthians 6:19,20).

Beginning again means rebuilding new hope into a life that has been broken by sorrow and defeat. It means getting on with the demands of life and embracing emotions in an honest way with the help of the Lord.

- You have the resources of Christ to forgive your ex-spouse and others who have hurt you (read Colossians 3:13).
- You have the strength to overcome temptation when you are living in the power of Christ (read Romans 13:14).
- You are free to be concerned with pleasing the Lord (read 1 Corinthians 7:32–35).
- You have shared in the sufferings of Christ and can be an effective example to others (read 1 Peter 4:19).

A fresh start requires turning eyes inward for deep personal growth. It demands rooting out all resentment to allow the Redeemer to restore your heart.

> *Though you have made me see troubles, many and bitter, you will restore my life again; from the depths of the earth you will again bring me up* (Psalm 71:20).

22

Loneliness

Longing to Belong

Dear June,

I am going through an adjustment after being separated from my spouse for about a year. I have to admit that I have caught myself seeking the wrong kind of comfort. I have been a Christian for a year, and I am overwhelmed with being alone. I don't seem to feel that I fit anywhere, not even with my Christian friends. How do Christians handle loneliness?

Dear Lonely,

There are many times when the feelings of loneliness become overwhelming, and being separated from a spouse is definitely one of these times. Your deep longing to belong and be comforted is natural because one of the basic needs God has placed within each of us is *security,* or the *need to belong*. Rather than trying to find a substitute to fill the void, you can use your loneliness as an opportunity to develop intimacy with the Lord in the midst of the pain. You said you have been a Christian for a year, so let me encourage you to *refocus* on your relationship with Christ, and then you will have the inner strength to *reach out* in love to those whom God will bring into your life.

Learn to Lean

Entrust your feelings of loneliness to the Lord.

God is trustworthy and intimately acquainted with your deepest inner feelings—pour out your heart to Him. "Trust in him at all times . . . pour out your hearts to him, for God is our refuge" (Psalm 62:8).

Expect God, not another person, to meet your needs.

Begin to depend on God and His promises to you. Feelings of rejection from a broken relationship often cause feelings of desolation and isolation. Periodically, people will reject you (that's a fact of life), but God will always accept you. He will never change; He is dependable. He promises to "meet all your needs according to his glorious riches in Christ Jesus" (Philippians 4:19).

Examine your heart and evaluate your actions.

Make Psalm 139:23,24 the prayer of your heart, "Search me, O God, and know my heart; test me and know my anxious thoughts. See if there is any offensive way in me, and lead me in the way everlasting."

Examining your heart can be a painful process, but it is a positive and necessary step in moving forward in your relationship with the Lord. Agree with God about your need to change some inappropriate behaviors and be honest before Him—He waits for you with open arms. Then pray, "Create in me a pure heart, O God, and renew a steadfast spirit within me" (Psalm 51:10).

Learn to Reach Out

Establish new relationships with other believers.

You are not alone in your loneliness—it is a condition experienced by many Christians—even many who are married. God did not create you to live in isolation, but rather to have fellowship with others. Initiate invitations to share a meal, to attend enjoyable events, or host a game night. Think of what types of activities you enjoy, make plans to do them, and include someone else who may be lonely. Everyone needs to have the support of loving friendships: "What a man desires is unfailing love" (Proverbs 19:22).

Express genuine interest in others.

Begin by accepting others just as they are. They may also be in great pain—as you become better acquainted, move beyond factual conversations to sharing feelings. Avoid complaining about your own situation and focus on becoming a positive encourager. Look for small ways to fill practical and spiritual needs of another person. "Each of you should look not only to your own interests, but also to the interests of others" (Philippians 2:4).

Extend His love to others—even when your own heart is needy.

Helping and reaching out to others in their time of need is one of the most powerful tools to defeat loneliness. Ask and expect the Lord to bring people of His choice into your life—people with whom you can build healthy, trusting, godly relationships. Make 2 Corinthians 1:3,4 your goal: "Praise be to the God and Father of our Lord Jesus Christ, the Father of compassion and the God of all comfort, who comforts us in all our troubles, so that we can comfort those in any trouble with the comfort we ourselves have received from God."

Even as you learn to walk with the Lord as your constant companion, there will be times of loneliness. Let me share some answers to questions you may periodically have when you feel lonely.

- *Question:* "My life is active and full. Why do I get lonely?"

Response: Activity alone is no cure for loneliness. Too many activities can be a numbing agent and actually deter the opportunity for growth.

Support: "My soul finds rest in God alone; my salvation comes from him" (Psalm 62:1).

- *Question:* "How do I deal with the guilt of feeling lonely when I have Christ in my heart?"

Response: It's not sin to have the pain of loneliness. We are made to have significant relationships with God and others. When there is great loss, there is great pain. Even Jesus hurt when His friend Lazarus died. Tears are not wrong; they are God-given.

Support: "Jesus wept" (John 11:35).

• *Question:* "Now that my mate is gone, what are the hardest times I will face?"

Response: The most emotional times will be holidays, birthdays, and anniversaries. Expect a period of grief. Grieving over a significant loss is a healthy and natural part of life.

Support: "[There is] a time to weep and a time to laugh, a time to mourn and a time to dance" (Ecclesiastes 3:4).

• *Question:* "How can I make it through the holidays?"

Response: Make plans to be with others on sentimental, special days; visit comforting family or friends or reach out to someone in need.

Support: "If one falls down, his friend can help him up. But pity the man who falls and has no one to help him up!" (Ecclesiastes 4:10).

• *Question:* "Does loneliness last forever?"

Response: No. One day, when we are with Him, there will be no more loneliness . . . no more death, no more mourning, no more tears.

Support: "He will wipe every tear from their eyes. There will be no more death or mourning or crying or pain, for the old order of things has passed away" (Revelation 21:4).

Loneliness is a fact of life in this fallen world. Although it can't always be alleviated, it can be *accepted*.

Learn to Belong

Since you were made to have an intimate relationship with God, your need for belonging is met through the presence of His Son living in you. As you seek to experience all He desires for you as His child, praise God with a thankful heart that He has chosen you to be with Him always. Then there is no question—you will find unending fulfillment and your heart will be deeply satisfied with the richness of God's unending love.

> *Find rest, O my soul, in God alone; my hope comes from him* (Psalm 62:5).

23

Single Parenting

Search for Security

Dear June,

I would like any help you have for single parenting. I am raising three children alone and it is such a struggle, both emotionally and financially. At times I feel like giving up, yet I know God doesn't want me to. Can you please help me?

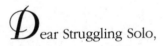

Dear Struggling Solo,

Someone once remarked that single parenting is the hardest job in the universe, and I'm sure you'd agree! Since more and more families are headed by a single parent, you are certainly not alone in your feelings. In a day when commitment means little, you are to be commended for honoring your God-given role as a parent. The Lord will support you, and I pray your children will grow to appreciate your high level of commitment to them.

God is intimately aware of your struggles as a single parent. His promise is to give you new strength and power as you place your hope in Him. Isaiah 40:29–31 says:

> He gives strength to the weary and increases the power of the weak. Even youths grow tired and weary, and young men stumble and fall; but those who hope in the LORD will renew their strength. They will soar on wings like eagles; they will run and not grow weary, they will walk and not be faint.

First, I want to address the two areas you mentioned in your letter which usually affect most everyone who raises children alone.

Financial Pressure

Money is one of the greatest concerns to single parents. Does it seem that, as your children grow taller, your wallet grows smaller? Costs for sports activities, social events, clothes—especially tennis shoes—add up quickly. Since financial responsibility is best learned through experience, let your children be aware of the family financial situation and involve them in the process of family budgeting. This helps meet their need to have more control over their lives and helps meet your need to be relieved of making all of the decisions in this area. Also, as they become involved in distinguishing needs from wants and in establishing priorities, you no longer bear that burden alone. If they're old enough for after-school jobs, you might establish a guideline dividing their earnings into giving, saving, necessities, and "extras."

Above all, remember God's promise in Philippians 4:19: "My God will meet all your needs according to his glorious riches in Christ Jesus." These are not hollow words. God's commitment to your family is strong and He is your Provider. Take to heart His financial principles:

Don't live on borrowed money.

Do set a budget and involve the children in planning. "Train a child in the way he should go, and when he is old he will not turn from it. The rich rule over the poor, and the borrower is servant to the lender" (Proverbs 22:6,7).

Don't take on the financial burden alone.

Do count on God to fulfill financial needs. "Look at the birds of the air; they do not sow or reap or store away in barns, and yet your heavenly Father feeds them. Are you not much more valuable than they?" (Matthew 6:26).

Don't shield your children from responsibilities.

Do give them household chores with daily, weekly, and monthly schedules. "Diligent hands will rule, but laziness ends in slave labor" (Proverbs 12:24).

Don't overcompensate by buying too much for your children.

Do realize you can't buy what your children need the most. "Better a little with the fear of the LORD than great wealth with turmoil. Better a meal of vegetables where there is love than a fattened calf with hatred" (Proverbs 15:16,17).

Emotional Overload

Feeling overwhelmed often occurs from the stress of single parenting. When you realize you cannot meet all of your children's needs you may feel guilty. This false guilt may compel you to play "Supermom," which leaves you with no time to yourself and on the brink of emotional burnout.

To break this vicious cycle, receive nurturing in a Bible study and surround yourself with other believers, especially those who have faced the problems you're facing. Hebrews 10:25 says, "Let us not give up meeting together, as some are in the habit of doing, but let us encourage one another—and all the more as you see the Day approaching."

Have you begun to recognize your pressures as God's tools to press you closer to Him? Just as you cannot meet all the needs of your children, don't expect them to meet your needs. The Lord wants to be your Need-Meeter. Take care of yourself by setting aside time to cultivate your personal relationship with the Lord and spend time with encouraging Christian friends. The degree to which you allow the Lord to fill you with a positive outlook toward your role determines the degree to which you can be successful as a single parent! These dos and don'ts will help alleviate your emotional overload.

Don't accept disrespect from your children.

> *Do realize that fear of rejection leads to passive parenting.* "Discipline your son, for in that there is hope; do not be a willing party to his death" (Proverbs 19:18).

Don't expect your children to fill your emotional needs.

> *Do nurture close friends for emotional support and role-modeling.* "He who walks with the wise grows

wise, but a companion of fools suffers harm" (Proverbs 13:20).

Don't criticize the absent parent.

Do mention the positive characteristics of the absent parent and, if possible, give children the opportunity to build a relationship with the absent parent. "Set a guard over my mouth, O LORD; keep watch over the door of my lips" (Psalm 141:3).

Don't think your children are "doomed."

Do know God has a plan for them and they can reach their full potential. " 'For I know the plans I have for you,' declares the LORD, 'plans to prosper you and not to harm you, plans to give you hope and a future' " (Jeremiah 29:11).

The Search for Security

For many, facing life as a single parent greatly threatens their deep, God-given, inner need for security. Once you have turned to the Lord and received His inner presence as your source of strength and eternal security, you become free to be God's instrument of temporary security for your children. As they sense your confidence and assurance, their world becomes a safer and healthier environment in which to grow and mature. A wise parent recognizes that all children need to feel secure more than they need material privilege or social advantage. Children raised by a single parent are more likely to have this inner need met if they can:

SECURITY

S*ee that you are emotionally healthy* (Psalm 146:5).

E*xperience a consistent and structured home life* (1 Corinthians 14:33).

C*ommunicate their true feelings without reproach* (Psalm 19:14).

U*nderstand they are in no way responsible for their situation* (Proverbs 16:22).

R*eceive a double portion of encouragement* (1 Thessalonians 2:11,12).

E*nter into a relationship with the Lord Jesus Christ* (Luke 18:16,17).

Don't Give Up!

You also wrote, "I feel like giving up, yet I know God doesn't want me to." You are so right to recognize that God doesn't want you to give up. Not only does He desire that you be the best you can be for your children, but He promises to be the strength you need to succeed. Claim Isaiah 41:10 as your personal promise as you look at the four final dos and don'ts: "Do not fear, for I am with you; do not be dismayed, for I am your God. I will strengthen you and help you; I will uphold you with my righteous right hand" (Isaiah 41:10).

Don't hang on to negative feelings and bitterness.

> *Do have a heart of thankfulness.* "Give thanks in all circumstances, for this is God's will for you in Christ Jesus" (1 Thessalonians 5:18).

Don't try to be both father and mother.

> *Do be the wisest parent possible in your God-given role.* "A father to the fatherless, a defender of widows, is God in his holy dwelling" (Psalm 68:5).

Don't look to the world for advice and approval.

> *Do look to God for correction and instruction.* "Search me, O God, and know my heart; test me and know my anxious thoughts. See if there is any offensive way in me, and lead me in the way everlasting" (Psalm 139:23,24).

Don't think you must remarry to receive help in parenting.

> *Do accept God's offer to meet your needs.* "For your Maker is your husband—the LORD Almighty is his name—the Holy One of Israel is your Redeemer; he is called the God of all the earth" (Isaiah 54:5).

***He** is always there for you* (Psalm 46:1).

***He** is a good listener* (Psalm 62:8).

***He** is faithful* (2 Timothy 2:13).

***He** is patient* (Psalm 86:15).

***He** is wise* (Job 12:13).

***He** is forgiving* (Psalm 30:5).

***He** loves you forever* (Jeremiah 31:3).

Never forget God the Father has a special heart for every single parent. If God in His infinite wisdom has given you the responsibility of raising a child alone, hold your head high—you have a high calling.

24

Singleness

One Is a Whole Number

Dear June,

For most of my life I have been lonely. I pray daily for God to bring me a mate, but it's very discouraging. I sometimes feel like Adam before God created Eve. I know God has the right person for me, but can you offer any advice or comfort in the meantime?

Dear "Adam,"

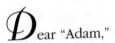

Let me share a freeing "math fact": Although you are not married, *you are not half a person. . . .* You are not an "incomplete" man wandering around just waiting for Wonder Woman to complete you. Although you may feel like a fraction, the fact is you are *one* person, and *one* is a whole number! What's more, according to the Bible, you are *complete* in Christ.

Comprehend Being Complete

When you humbled your heart, turned from self-centered sin, and received Jesus Christ as your Lord and Savior, you received the very presence of God to indwell you. This is no small matter. With "Christ in you" (Colossians 1:27), you received the most precious Companion of all—the indwelling Christ, whose inner presence promises to fulfill you. In the Phillips translation, Colossians 2:9,10 says, "It is in him [Christ] that God gives a full and complete expression of himself . . . moreover, your own completeness is realized in him." It's really true, you are *complete* in Christ.

Challenge Your Conclusions

Although nothing more is needed to complete you, obviously you don't *feel* complete. I sense your deep state of loneliness—which is not just the temporary loneliness everyone periodically experiences. Because you have asked for advice, let me point out that *feeling follows thinking*. If you *think* lonely thoughts, you will *feel* lonely emotions. If you *think* sad thoughts, you will *feel* sad emotions. Likewise, if you *think* grateful thoughts, you will *feel* grateful emotions. Romans 12:2 explains that you are "transformed by the renewing of your mind."

Most people are not aware that *they have a choice* about how they feel. They assume that their emotions are powerless pawns in the chess game of acceptance and rejection. Since you don't like the way you feel (lonely and discouraged), and since what you feel is based on what you think, ask yourself, "What have I been thinking?" Then challenge those lonely, discouraging conclusions with God's truth: "Since I am complete in Christ, I will choose to be content."

Choose to be Content

Contentment is more than a feeling—it is a learned and disciplined state of mind. In Philippians 4:11 of the Amplified version of the Bible, the apostle Paul, who was also single, said, "I have learned how to be content (satisfied to the point where I am not disturbed or disquieted) in whatever state I am." Contentment comes from making daily, minute-by-minute choices to live in dependence on Jesus Christ. Know that you really can be content. Contentment for singles is not a fantasy. It can be your reality if you act on these choices.

CONTENT

C*onfess the difficulty to God.* Don't try to ignore or deny your feelings. (Stuffed feelings won't go away.) Temporary feelings of loneliness and discouragement are natural and normal. In fact, all married partners could tell you about times of deep loneliness within their marriages. Bring your fears and frustration to Jesus. He alone understands the depth of your loneliness. "We do not have a high priest who is unable to sympathize with our weaknesses, but we have one [Jesus] who has been tempted in every way, just as we are—yet was without sin. Let us then approach the throne of grace with confidence, so that we may receive mercy and find grace to help us in our time of need" (Hebrews 4:15,16).

Lord, you know my heart. I admit that . . .

O*pen your heart to singleness.* See this season of singleness as a *gift* from God. If God allows you to be single for whatever period of time, His plan is to use that season to grow both you and those around you in ways otherwise not possible. The apostle Paul said, "It is good for a man not to marry. . . . I wish that all men were as I am. But each man has his own gift from God" (1 Corinthians 7:1,7). Paul's reasoning was that single adults are less distracted in life and can give "undivided devotion to the Lord" (1 Corinthians 7:35). As he traveled unencumbered, Paul's gift of singleness was used to draw others to Christ. Ultimately, he became the greatest missionary of all time. Wait on the Lord to reveal His will for your singleness and, while you wait, look for little ways in which He would want to use you (such as teaching a Sunday school class or tutoring).

Lord, help me to see my singleness as a gift. For whatever time I am single, I want to be used by You. May I see needs around me and be open to meeting those needs.

N*ix the "greener grass" comparison.* Don't assume, "I'd be happy if only I were married." Marriage can't guarantee happiness, much less life without heartaches. In 1 Corinthians 7:28 Paul explains, "Those who marry will face many troubles in this life, and I want to spare you this." Realize that married couples experience disappointment, discouragement, and disillusionment—even divorce. The grass is not always greener in someone else's backyard!

Lord, keep me from the "if only's" in life and from comparing myself with those who are married. Teach me what it really means to be content.

Thank God for His sovereign purpose. Look at your longings, and then thank God for how He will use those longings in your life. God's ultimate purpose is to conform you to the character of Christ. Romans 8:28,29 says: "In all things God works for the good of those who love him. . . . For those God foreknew he also predestined to be conformed to the likeness of his Son." How does He make you more Christlike? Just as Jesus was dependent on His Father to meet His needs, the Father will teach you to depend on Jesus to meet your needs. Most often this deeper dependence is developed through deeper disappointments. He may allow discouragement in your close relationships so that you will stop being so dependent upon others and allow Him to be your Need-Meeter. At times, He will do this solely through His intimate relationship with you and at other times He will work through the love and lives of others. Above all, *He* wants to be your *source* for the love, significance, and security you so desire.

Lord, I don't want to have a misplaced dependency on others. Instead of looking to people to meet my needs, I want to look to You to be my Need-Meeter.

Evaluate the positives of singleness. Have you thanked God for your advantages? Philippians 4:8 states, "Whatever is true, whatever is noble, whatever is right, whatever is pure, whatever is lovely, whatever is admirable—if anything is excellent or praiseworthy—think about such things." Enjoy what you do have, and verbally thank God for your greater freedom:

- to help and serve others
- to change your schedule abruptly
- to do your own financial planning and spending
- to accept travel opportunities
- to spend time alone
- to nurture several deep relationships
- to serve the Lord with undivided devotion

Lord, thank You that because I am single, I have more freedom to . . .

Nurture a "family of friends." Notice that, although Jesus was single, He had a family of friends. While some were closer than others, He spent both quality and quantity time with a number of meaningful friends. God wants you to have significant friendships. In fact, Scripture emphasizes the importance of friendship. The comfort of friendship is revealed in Proverbs 17:17, "A friend loves at all times." The helpfulness of friendship is shared in Proverbs 27:9, "The pleasantness of one's friend springs from his earnest counsel." The growth through friendship is seen in Proverbs 13:20, "He who walks with the wise grows wise." Ask God for friends with whom you have the same spiritual foundation. Pray for and cultivate healthly friendships:

- Ask God to give you wise and faithful friends.
- Nurture several quality friendships—not just one.
- Attend a weekly Bible study.

- Initiate calls to potential friends—don't wait to be called.
- Invite others to your home.
- Ask questions and share on the "feeling" level.
- Listen with focused attention.
- Schedule quality talking times at least every week or two.
- Look for humor and find ways to have fun!

Lord, may I have Your choice of friends for my life. Instead of focusing on what I will get from them, may I focus on what I can give to them.

***T**rust your future to the Father.* Your singleness is not a surprise to God. Before you were born, He planned your life with a purpose. Now the question is, Are you willing to trust Him with your singleness? If so, how?

- Allow the Lord to chart your course. Jeremiah 10:23 says, "I know, O LORD, that a man's life is not his own; it is not for man to direct his steps."
- Memorize Jeremiah 29:11, " 'For I know the plans I have for you,' declares the LORD, 'plans to prosper you and not to harm you, plans to give you hope and a future.' "
- Find weekly fellowship in a Christ-centered church which teaches from the Bible: "Let us not give up meeting together, as some are in the habit of doing, but let us encourage one another" (Hebrews 10:25).

- Walk through doors of opportunity that God opens in your heart, such as further schooling, a photography course, volunteer work, a hobby, short-term missions. "Forget the former things; do not dwell on the past. See, I am doing a new thing! Now it springs up; do you not perceive it? I am making a way in the desert and streams in the wasteland" (Isaiah 43:18,19).

Lord, if I dwell on my past hurts, I will miss Your present purpose for my singleness. I'm willing to trust You with my future. . . . I trust You with my life.

Let me add a word of caution: Guard your heart from absorbing the unbiblical attitudes of others. Some misguided "marrieds" infer that "singles" are merely second-class citizens. They suggest that singles aren't serious about life and can't make commitments. Somehow they seem to forget that spiritual giants like Elijah, Daniel, and Paul were all single. And Jesus Himself was single, with a single-minded mission. He did not fret over His preferred wants—He focused on His Father's will.

Regardless of why you are single or how long you have been single, discard discontent . . . choose to be content. Delight in the freedom that you do have—after all, it is a gift from God.

Godliness with contentment is great gain (1 Timothy 6:6).

PART 6

Seasons of Sorrow

25

Abortion

Making the Right Choice

Dear June,

I have recently found out that my thirteen-year-old daughter is six months pregnant. We are in great need of counseling through the mail. My wife (who is separated from me) told me that she would encourage our daughter to get an abortion. I told her, "No, no, that is not God's will. It is murder. She might not survive!" Please, please pray hard, with all your heart. . . .

Dear Distraught Dad,

What a heartbreaking situation you and your family are experiencing but how wonderful that your daughter has a father such as you to give her loving support. Your brokenness is apparent from the tone of your letter, so the first word I want to say is, "There is nothing too big or too out of control that our great God cannot redeem and heal." He delights in healing the broken heart when we give Him all the pieces.

Psalm 34:18 says, "The LORD is close to the brokenhearted and saves those who are crushed in spirit."

Please know how very special your daughter is to God, as is the precious life she is carrying within her. Also be assured that God cares for you and will be with you during these difficult days. He is your refuge and your strength. This turn of events has not caught Him by surprise. He has already gone before you and your daughter and has prepared the perfect way you are both to walk. While your situation may appear hopeless, claim this promise:

> "I know the plans I have for you," declares the LORD, "plans to prosper you and not to harm you, plans to give you hope and a future. Then you will call upon me and come and pray to me, and I will listen to you. You will seek me and find me when you seek me with all your heart. I will be found by you . . ." (Jeremiah 29:11–14).

Ask the Lord to use you as an extension of His love, grace, and mercy within your daughter's life. Most likely, she is frightened and ashamed. Help her concentrate on God's love and forgiveness and on His special plan for her and the new life inside her. Help her understand that abortion is against God's plan. Abortion does immense harm to everyone involved. I believe if people were truly aware of the long-term effects of abortion, they would never consider it as an option.

I encourage you to become involved in your daughter's life in a practical and dependable way. If she is living with her mother, do not defy your wife's authority, but consider taking some steps that need immediate attention as each of you face this crisis.

- *Prayerfully commit your daughter and her baby to the Lord's keeping.*
- *Express to your daughter how special both she and her baby are to you and to God.* Tell her you love her regardless of the situation. Reassure her that she is not alone.
- *If you are financially able, let your daughter know you will take care of her and the baby during this time.* If you cannot, then make other arrangements. Perhaps she would be comfortable with another family member—someone who would be willing and able to care for her. Offer to contribute as much as you can toward her expenses. You can also contact your local church for information on homes for unwed mothers.
- *Find someone within the medical community who can clearly and compassionately take her step-by-step through the various stages of her pregnancy.* It is important that she be given as much information as she can understand and process—especially about what is going on within her body. The more she knows, the more secure she will be, thus fewer surprises to catch her off guard or make her fearful.
- *Explain to your daughter that adoption is a caring option for her unborn child.* While there are staggering numbers of abortions annually, there are still

more families seeking to adopt a child each year. Many adoption agencies will cover all medical costs and any counseling your daughter might need. She can ensure that her child is placed in a loving Christian home. Remind her that Moses was given up for adoption and became one of the greatest spiritual leaders of all times.

- *Seek outside counsel with a pastor or a counselor for you and your daughter.* Your daughter will need to work through many confusing feelings. You will also need to know how best to love and support her in this process. Remember, there will be lifelong ramifications with whatever decisions you and your daughter make. While it is true that her life will never be the same, God will be faithful to her and will bring good to her out of this situation.

Your relationship with your wife is also crucial at this time. You have no control over her, but you can control the way in which you respond to her. Put your differences behind you and seek to communicate with her. Most importantly *pray for your wife faithfully:* "As for me, far be it from me that I should sin against the LORD by failing to pray for you" (1 Samuel 12:23).

Ask the Lord for wisdom and sensitivity in your interactions with your wife. Also, pray that she would have God's heart and, thus, a changed heart toward the unborn child. Your wife probably feels devastated, guilty, and overwhelmed with responsibility and in need of emotional support herself. Come alongside her as much as you can and be there for her. Pray that the Lord will use the present set of circumstances to bind the two of you together to bring a measure of healing to your relationship. Remember, a crisis can bring cohesion or a chasm, depending on how it is handled.

Many people have had changed hearts toward abortion after seeing God's heart on children in the womb. I encourage you to share verbally and in writing God's principles on the sanctity of life. Become familiar with the following points and be ready to speak confidently with your wife and your daughter, giving the reasons for the assurance that is in you.

> Always be prepared to give an answer to everyone who asks you to give the reason for the hope that you have. But do this with gentleness and respect (1 Peter 3:15).

Human life begins at conception.

> For you [God] created my inmost being; you knit me together in my mother's womb (Psalm 139:13).

The little one inside the womb of a mother is a person.

> My frame was not hidden from you when I was made in the secret place. When I was woven together in the depths of the earth, your eyes saw my unformed body. All the days ordained for me were written in your book before one of them came to be (Psalm 139:15,16).

A woman has a right to control over her own body. However, she doesn't have the right to kill her unborn child who is a separate person within her body and who has a God-ordained call and destiny.

> Before I [God] formed you in the womb I knew you, before you were born I set you apart . . . (Jeremiah 1:5).

The Old Testament law gave the same legal value to an unborn child as to an adult.

> If men who are fighting hit a pregnant woman and she gives birth prematurely but there is no serious injury, the offender must be fined whatever the woman's husband demands and the court allows. But if there is serious injury, you are to take life for life (Exodus 21:22,23).

If a mother is concerned about her baby being handicapped or deformed, assure her that God has special plans for her baby and will glorify Himself through her child.

> He [Jesus] saw a man blind from birth. His disciples asked him, "Rabbi, who sinned, this man or his parents, that he was born blind?" "Neither this man nor his parents sinned," said Jesus, "but this happened so that the work of God might be displayed in his life" (John 9:1–3).

God's principles should never be sacrificed for emotional, financial, or any kind of manmade arguments.

> There is a way that seems right to a man, but in the end it leads to death (Proverbs 14:12).

An unborn child is innocent of wrongdoing. And, since there is no guilt by due process of law to legally justify the death penalty, abortion is murder.

> You shall not murder (Exodus 20:13).

God commands you to take action against killing the innocent.

> Rescue those being led away to death; hold back those staggering toward slaughter. If you say, "But we knew nothing about this," does not he who weighs the heart perceive it? Does not he who guards your life know it? Will he not repay each person according to what he has done? (Proverbs 24:11–12).

God, the Giver of Life, commands everyone to believe in the sanctity of life and to choose life.

> I have set before you life and death, blessings and curses. Now choose life, so that you and your children may live (Deuteronomy 30:19).

My prayer is that you, as a father, will continue to reflect the heart of the heavenly Father. As a provider and protecter, may you have a strong, yet tender influence on your precious daughter so that she will have the courage to choose life!

26

Grief

From Sorrow to Strength

Dear June,

I am overwhelmed at this point in my life. Three weeks ago, my dad very suddenly went home to be with the Lord. He was 69 years old and was generally healthy. When I think of the things my dad won't see (like our children and "special occasions"), I feel very sad. The thing is, I don't understand why it happened so suddenly. I feel as though I may fall apart. I feel so lonely without my father—I already miss him so much. Please pray for me during this time. I need it badly.

Dear Overwhelmed,

The loss of a dearly loved parent *is* overwhelming. It seems we all know that death is inevitable, but when it happens we are caught unaware. Sadness and sorrow become lead weights in our hearts, crushing the joy and optimism of life. This is especially true when death occurs unexpectedly and we become consumed with the question, "Why?" The painful feelings you have are normal and have not caught God by surprise. Through grief He can enter your heart more intimately. It can be a doorway to emotional growth and deep spiritual awareness of the abiding presence of God: "The LORD is close to the brokenhearted and saves those who are crushed in spirit" (Psalm 34:18).

Your Grief Is Good

Not only is it natural to experience sadness at the death of someone you deeply love, it is also natural for you (the one who is left behind) to go through a grieving process. This process is a change that occurs step-by-step until you reach a place of emotional healing. But God is with you! "And our hope for you is firm, because we know that just as you share in our sufferings, so also you share in our comfort" (2 Corinthians 1:7). Also remember, "Weeping may remain for a night, but rejoicing comes in the morning" (Psalm 30:5).

The length of the journey and the emotional swings that accompany your grief will vary. The time it takes to heal could extend from six months to three years or, in some cases, substantially longer. For this reason, I encourage you not to compare your experience with that of someone else. Even though others are also experiencing the loss of your father, your loss is unique to you. It is based on the individual personal relationship you had with your father. Additionally, your emotional, mental, and spiritual makeup are exclusively yours and play a part in the grief process as well.

Be aware of the tendency to focus on what you *will not have,* thus losing the enjoyment of the wonderful memories you *do have.* This negative mind-set is a great temptation when the loss is sudden. Let your perspective be, "Look at the years I *did have my father* in my life. . . . I have many great memories for which I am thankful." Psalm 100:4 tells us that we can "enter his gates with thanksgiving and his courts with praise." This implies that a thankful heart moves more quickly into the comforting presence of God. In the midst of your pain, let this be the opportunity for your heavenly Father to fill the empty loneliness. It is my sincere prayer that you will be able to quickly find that comfort.

Your Comfort Is Christ

C*ome to the God of comfort.*

Believe that God knows and understands your pain, and then ask Him to heal the emptiness you feel. "O LORD my God, I called to you for help and you healed me" (Psalm 30:2). The sweetest and most complete healing comes from the hand of God.

O*pen your heart to the reality of pain.*

When a loved one dies, there sometimes is a tendency to blame God for the loss. Remember, God is loving. He did not allow your father to die in order to punish you or to cause you pain. Death is a reality for all of us. But God promises to walk closely with us when we must experience the loss of a loved one or when we face death ourselves: "Even though I walk through the valley of the shadow of death, I will fear no evil, for you are with me; your rod and your staff, they comfort me" (Psalm 23:4).

***M**aintain a clear conscience.*

Often our grief is mixed with guilt. We mourn over things done or things left undone. This is especially true when a loved one dies unexpectedly. If there are any broken promises, unkind words, or inappropriate actions which continue to haunt your conscience, confess it to the Lord, which literally means "agree with." Remember, once you have confessed your sins, "he is faithful and just and will forgive us our sins and purify us from all unrighteousness" (1 John 1:9).

***F**ind your strength in Christ.*

You may be feeling that your grief is too great to overcome. This is a good place to be, for we are blessed when we discover our own weaknesses. God knows we are frail, and that is why He has given us His Son, Jesus Christ, to be our inner source of strength. When you feel as though you "may fall apart," claim Philippians 4:13, "I can do everything through him who gives me strength."

***O**btain comfort from those whom God sends to you.*

Though you can never replace the loss of your father, it will help to lessen your pain if you share your feelings with one or more of the significant people in your life. Don't think you must hide your pain or your tears. God says, "Carry each other's burdens, and in this way you will fulfill the law of Christ" (Galatians 6:2). Make time for strengthening your existing relationships by opening your heart to trustworthy, caring individuals. Now is the season for drawing comfort and support from those whom God places around you. Nothing else binds people together like sharing a painful experience.

***R**einforce your faith by giving comfort to others.*

Second Corinthians 1:3–5 says this best: "Praise be to the God and Father of our Lord Jesus Christ, the Father of compassion and the God of all comfort, who comforts us in all our troubles, so that we can comfort those in any trouble with the comfort we ourselves have received from God. For just as the sufferings of Christ flow over into our lives, so also through Christ our comfort overflows."

***T**reasure the positives.*

True to God's Word, there is a rainbow that follows the storms of life. Experiencing godly sorrow enlarges our hearts with more compassion for others. We seem to develop a greater acceptance and appreciation for people and the world around us. As you begin to see a new purpose in life and a new hope for the future, you will "have learned to be content whatever the circumstances" (Philippians 4:11).

Your Strength Comes Through Sorrow

God, through Jesus Christ, is your greatest hope. I encourage you to lean all of your being onto the Lord during these days, for He dearly loves you. He will supply you with all you need to endure the darkest hours. Hebrews 6:19 reminds us, "We have this hope as an anchor for the soul, firm and secure." Take this promise and turn it into a prayer:

> *Thank You, Lord, that You have given me an anchor for my soul. Through Your presence I will move from my sorrow to Your strength.*

27

Premarital Pregnancy

Enough Love for Two

Dear June,

I'm going to have a child out of wedlock. I feel I've not only let my God down, but also my family and myself. Will I ever find the inner peace that everything will be okay? This is a very shameful and dark part of my life. Is this pregnancy God's punishment for my sin? Has His perspective of me changed?

I'm ready to follow God wherever He leads, yet I wonder, will my life ever get back to normal? It doesn't seem fair that the father's not here and that I am the only one suffering. How do I fill the void of a father figure in my house?

June, I'm scared for my child and what lies ahead. What is the most important thing I can do to give my child enough love for two?

Dear Scared,

Although you fear the future, I sense your love and care for your child. Let me commend you for letting your unborn see the light of life. Rest assured that God never forms a life without a purpose for that life. Years ago the Lord said to Jeremiah, "Before I formed you in the womb I knew you, before you were born I set you apart . . ." (1:5). That means God has a plan and a purpose for both you and the child in your womb. So don't be scared, for the Lord has said,

> I know the plans I have for you . . . plans to prosper you and not to harm you, plans to give you hope and a future (Jeremiah 29:11).

Each question you have as an expectant mother is very important. Let's look at them one at a time.

"Has God's perspective of me changed?"

No, your pregnancy did not take God by surprise. The Bible says, "With the Lord . . . a thousand years are like a day" (2 Peter 3:8). All along, God knew you would be expecting this child. So how does He see you? Simply put, you are dearly loved, but because you have sinned and will continue to sin, you will always need the Savior. The most well-known New Testament passage reveals God's heart for you:

> For God so *loved* the world that he gave his one and only Son, that whoever believes in him shall not perish but have eternal life. For God did not send his Son into the world to condemn the world, but to *save the world* through him (John 3:16,17, emphasis added).

Obviously, God's perspective of you is born out of compassion, not condemnation. Therefore, your heavenly Father has already met your need in two different respects. You not only needed Christ to save you from the *penalty* of sin (eternal hell), but now you also need Him to save you from the *pull* of sin (earthly habits). How will He do that? When you gave your life to Jesus Christ, you received "Christ *in* you" (Colossians 1:27), so today His empowering presence continually "saves" you from that pull. (Read Romans 6.)

"Will I ever have inner peace?"

Yes, you will find peace, although you will always experience problems. Remember, no problem is too big for God to solve. As the *Prince of Peace,* Jesus wants to *be peace* for you. Regardless of the problem, you can have *His* inner peace because of *His* inner presence. Jesus said:

> In me you may have peace. In this world you will have trouble. But take heart! I have overcome the world (John 16:33).

"Is this pregnancy God's punishment?"

No, this pregnancy is a *consequence of sin,* not a punishment for sin. God will use the consequences of sin to draw you into a deeper dependency on Him. Although you made a mistake, *your child is not a mistake.* This unborn child is a precious creation of God. Just like David, who sang to the Lord in the psalms, your little one could say to the Lord:

> You created my inmost being; you knit me together in my mother's womb. I praise you because I am fearfully and wonderfully made; your works are wonderful, I know that full well. My frame was not hidden from you when I was made in the secret place. When I was woven together in the depths of the earth, your eyes saw my unformed body. All the days ordained for me were written in your book before one of them came to be (Psalm 139:13–16).

"Will my life ever get back to normal?"

No, you will never go back to your life as you once knew it. Your unborn child is permanently changing your perspectives, plans, and priorities. You can't get back to your "previous normal."

However, once your child is born and you both settle into a routine, you will establish a "new normal," although this will take many months. In the meantime let this Scripture take on a special meaning for you:

> Forget the former things; do not dwell on the past. See, I am doing a new thing! Now it springs up; do you not perceive it? I am making a way in the desert and streams in the wasteland (Isaiah 43:18,19).

"Why am I the only one suffering?"

Don't become bitter about the birth father's abandoning his rightful role and responsibilities. Although you can't see any consequences for him, don't think they don't exist. In His own time and way the Lord will deal with the child's father. You have this assurance, "Do not take revenge, my friends, but leave room for God's wrath, for it is written: 'It is mine to avenge; I will repay,' says the Lord" (Romans 12:19).

Acknowledge your *legitimate* anger. Then give up your right to stay angry—release it to the Lord. Ephesians 4:26 says, " 'In your anger do not sin': Do not let the sun go down while you are still angry." Each time you think of the father of your child, choose to forgive him again and again. Be aware that a lack of forgiveness will harden your heart and produce bitter fruit which could poison your child. "See to it . . . that no bitter root grows up to cause trouble and defile many" (Hebrews 12:15).

"How do I fill the void of a father figure in my house?"

You need not (and cannot) be both mother *and* father. God did not design you physically to be a father. Just be the best mom you can be and let the heavenly Father play His unique role. In the drama of life, David specifically calls the Lord, "a father to the fatherless" (Psalm 68:5). That is the compassionate part God promises to play . . . and there could be no better Father!

> But you, O God, do see trouble and grief; you consider it to take it in hand. The victim commits himself to you; you are the helper of the fatherless (Psalm 10:14).

You can certainly request that male family members and friends become involved with your child. But don't be deeply disappointed if they quickly forget because, in reality, your need is not their need. Therefore, when raising your child, reinforce the "father" image of God with:

- Scriptures of His guidance such as Psalm 25:4,5.
- songs of His sovereignty such as Psalm 59:17.
- words of His watch-care such as Psalm 121.
- prayers for His provision such as Philippians 4:19.

"He's Got the Whole World in His Hands" means He's got your baby too!

"How can I give my child enough love for two?"

By yourself, you can't—you are only one person. Oh, you can certainly help your child feel secure with much holding and hugging, singing and smiling, caressing and kissing. And you will want to provide loving environments (a Sunday school nursery, sensitive neighborhood friends). Still, *you are only one person.*

Yet in another respect, you can "give your child enough love for two" if you secure your little one in the love of God.

- Share the everlasting love of God (see Jeremiah 31:3).
- Sing the truth of "Jesus Loves Me" (see John 3:16).
- Speak memory verses like "God is love" (see 1 John 4:16).
- Study and present God's saving love (see 1 John 3:1).

Even now, claim this psalm for yourself, then turn it into a prayer:

> The LORD will fulfill his purpose for me; your love, O LORD, endures forever—do not abandon the works of your hands (Psalm 138:8).

"I'm scared!"

Being scared is understandable. You are challenged with major changes—not just physical, but social and emotional. Although you should expect insensitivity from some, remember that those who throw the most dirt are the ones who lose the most ground! But with Christ in you, you can:

- Speak well of those who hurt you (Romans 12:14).
- Forgive those who grieve you (Colossians 3:13).
- Love those who are against you (Matthew 5:44a).
- Pray for those who persecute you (Matthew 5:44b).

Regardless of the rejection you may receive from others, don't expect Jesus to reject you. During His earthly life He loved sinners. . . . That is why they were so drawn to Him. Not because He told them how bad they were—they already knew that—but because He showed them how loved they were. Such love moved their hearts and changed their lives.

> There is no fear in love. But perfect love drives out fear, because fear has to do with punishment. The man who fears is not made perfect in love (1 John 4:18).

Do you know how perfectly Jesus loves *you?* In John 8 you can see His love laced with compassion. The judgmental Jewish leaders asked Jesus if, according to the law, they should stone a woman caught in adultery. His poignant reply was, "If any of you is without sin, let him be the first to throw a stone at her" (verse 7). Slowly, one by one, they all slithered away. Then Jesus handed this woman the cup of compassion, "Neither do I condemn you. . . . Go now and leave your life of sin" (verse 11). To Jesus, the concern was not her sin, but her soul. She needed a changed life . . . His life. He is handing you this same cup of compassion, and you have responded with your life—a changed life that has more than enough love for two.

> *So do not fear, for I am with you; do not be dismayed, for I am your God. I will strengthen you and help you; I will uphold you with my righteous right hand* (Isaiah 41:10).

28

Terminal Illness

Life-and-Death Dilemma

Dear June,

My fifteen-year-old daughter has leukemia. She was scheduled to come off the chemotherapy treatment two weeks ago, but the doctors said they don't think she will survive if she does. They want her to stay on the treatment, but she refuses. She argues that the last time she went back on treatment (eighteen months ago), we promised her if it came up again we would let her make the decision.

I am so torn, I don't know what to do! If I make her take the chemotherapy and she relapses anyhow (which she has done before) and dies, I will feel the blame. If I don't make her take it and she dies, I will still feel the blame. I know the Bible says God won't allow more to be put on me than I can bear, but at this point I feel this is more than I can handle.

The selfish side of me says, "Make her take the treatment, because I want her with me." My compassionate side says, "She's been through enough" (nine years of treatment). I'm in a no-win situation. I am a Christian and I love the Lord, but sometimes I wonder, "Does He really care, and if He does, why doesn't He do something?"

Dear No-Win,

Your situation is indeed heartbreaking as you confront these extremely painful decisions. Coming face-to-face with your own child's potential death has to be a parent's worst nightmare and greatest fear. It is understandable that you feel no one can comprehend your pain . . . not even God. But my heart cries out to assure you that God does know—and He greatly cares. He has set a limit on how difficult your circumstances can become. He measures and weighs every heartache. Just as He sees each tiny sparrow that falls to the ground, He is watching over you! "So don't be afraid; you are worth more than many sparrows" (Matthew 10:31).

As difficult as it may be right now, it is critical that you trust the Lord's sovereignty in your circumstances. Eighteen months ago when you promised your daughter that she could make her own decision, God knew what her condition would be today. Nothing concerning your daughter's illness has taken Him by surprise. The reality is, your daughter's life does not hinge on your decision or on her decision but on God's design and purpose for her life. You see, He is the one who planned a divine purpose for her, establishing her days before she was ever born and then knitting her together in your womb.

> You created my inmost being; you knit me together in my mother's womb. I praise you because I am

> fearfully and wonderfully made; your works are wonderful, I know that full well. My frame was not hidden from you when I was made in the secret place. When I was woven together in the depths of the earth, your eyes saw my unformed body. All the days ordained for me were written in your book before one of them came to be (Psalm 139:13–16).

What does hinge on your decision is your relationship with your daughter. Therefore, I encourage you to honor your word to your daughter and trust her choice and her life to God. Then focus on deepening your relationship with her, building it on the relationship you both have with God. Spend time together reading and discussing God's Word, praying, and praising God. Share spiritual insights and make special memories. Clear up any grievances which may exist between the two of you and keep a clear conscience before her and God. Delight in her as your heavenly Father delights in you.

Of course, it is difficult to let go of your daughter, but you can find comfort in the fact that *she is ultimately in God's hands* and as much as you love her, He loves her much more perfectly. Just as God asked Abraham to trust Him with his beloved son Isaac, God is now asking you to trust Him with your beloved daughter. And, although Isaac's life was spared, it was God that spared it, not Abraham. In Abraham's heart, Isaac was already dead when he placed Isaac on the altar of sacrifice and raised the knife over his body. Abraham knew God was trustworthy and it was for him to obey God rather than try to play God. (Read Genesis 22:1–18 and Hebrews 11:17–19.) I pray that, like Abraham, you will release your child's life into God's loving care and experience God's sweet peace and comfort as promised to you in Matthew 11:28,29:

> Come to me, all you who are weary and burdened, and I will give you rest. Take my yoke upon you and learn from me, for I am gentle and humble in heart, and you will find rest for your souls.

Please be aware that many people in a situation like yours feel *false guilt*. True guilt is based on having done something contrary to what God would want. False guilt, on the other hand, is based not on having done something wrong but on wrongly assuming responsibility for something. Should your daughter decide to discontinue treatment, you are not responsible for her choice and much less responsible should she die. "The LORD brings death and makes alive; he brings down to the grave and raises up" (1 Samuel 2:6). (See "Guilt" under Part 1 for more information on true and false guilt.)

To face the eventuality of death, for ourselves and our loved ones, is a difficult assignment for most of us. It seems we stay helplessly blind to how scantily thin the curtain is that separates this life from the next—until God brings us out of the audience and places us onto His stage of reality. Since reality is the essence of truth, God's promise is still the same . . . "Then you will know the truth, and the truth will set you free" (John 8:32). The following are three scriptural truths which bring us all comfort when facing death.

Death Is Designed

Embracing the God-given gift of life means inheriting death. The first breath of life is the first step toward death. One of the characteristics of spiritual maturity is recognizing and accepting death as a natural part of God's design. "There is a time for everything, and a season for every activity under heaven: a time to be born and a time to die" (Ecclesiastes 3:1–2).

Death Is a Doorway

Death can be a doorway to a more abundant eternal life or it can be the gateway to eternal misery. Death is not an end to life but a new beginning. Since we are born with a heart's desire to live forever, only faith can reach out and embrace God's promise of eternal life. "Enter through the narrow gate. For wide is the gate and broad is the road that leads to destruction, and many enter through it. But small is the gate and narrow the road that leads to life, and only a few find it" (Matthew 7:13,14).

Death Is Divine

The reality is that all Christians have already died! God's desire for you as His child is "death to self" and submission to the divine life of Christ living within you, expressing His life through you. "I have been crucified with Christ and I no longer live, but Christ lives in me. The life I live in the body, I live by faith in the Son of God, who loved me and gave himself for me" (Galatians 2:20).

If there is any question as to where your daughter will spend eternity, then spend time specifically talking with her about this. If you don't feel comfortable doing this, ask someone else whom she respects to help her understand how to come into a personal relationship with Jesus Christ. She needs to be aware of the consequences of this life-and-death decision.

When days are difficult and grief takes its toll, take comfort in your Bible by looking up these truths. Meditate on them, memorize them, and maintain God's perspective on the human dilemma of life and death.

- Your life is not your own. You belong to God and can rest in the assurance that He will act with total fairness and love toward you and your daughter—in life and in death. "If we live, we live to the Lord; and if we die, we die to the Lord. So, whether we live or die, we belong to the Lord" (Romans 14:8).
- The specialness of life is not in the length of life, but in the quality of life. "Now as always Christ will be exalted in my body, whether by life or by death. For to me, to live is Christ and to die is gain" (Philippians 1:20,21).
- God never lets anything happen to us that doesn't have a purpose. "Many are the plans in a man's heart, but it is the LORD's purpose that prevails" (Proverbs 19:21).
- God never gives us more than we can bear. He will provide a way out so that you can stand up under

it. "No temptation has seized you except what is common to man. And God is faithful; he will not let you be tempted beyond what you can bear. But when you are tempted, he will also provide a way out so that you can stand up under it (1 Corinthians 10:13).

- God is in control. Nothing in life or death can occur until it has first passed through the fingers of our loving Lord. "See now that I myself am He! There is no god besides me. I put to death and I bring to life, I have wounded and I will heal, and no one can deliver out of my hand" (Deuteronomy 32:39).
- Every child of God is going to a place much better than anything offered here. We sometimes have an earthly perspective on life and feel that staying here would be better, but in God's eyes, heaven would be best. "He will wipe every tear from their eyes. There will be no more death or mourning or crying or pain, for the old order of things has passed away" (Revelation 21:4).

You have had a long, difficult trial, being at your daughter's side through this illness and its many treatments. I would like to share a poem with you that was written around the text in 2 Corinthians 12:7–10. Paul pleaded three times for God to remove the thorn of suffering from his life. Yet when God's answer was, "My grace is sufficient for you, for my power is made perfect in weakness," Paul found that his suffering was his blessing because he was:

Learning to Lean

Just to keep my heart humble,
    God allowed this deep pain.
'Twas a part of affliction,
    No relief could I gain.
All my pleas for a miracle
    Brought this word from above:
In your weakness is power;
    It's My pathway of love.
Now the "why's" are all silent,
    For His truth I have seen.
I shall rest in my weakness,
    And on Christ I will lean.

PART 7

Growing in Grace

29

Forgiveness

Mission Possible

Dear June,

I had a very rough childhood filled with lots of rejection. My parents divorced when I was young and neither parent wanted me. I was pawned off on different relatives and finally ended up with my grandmother. That was so many years ago, and both of my parents have since passed away. However, I still find it impossible to forgive them for what they did. I'm frustrated. What should I do?

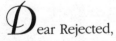

Dear Rejected,

You have obviously faced immense rejection in your life—rejection so painful that you've felt forgiveness was impossible. While it's true you have felt unwanted, what is not true is that you have no ability to forgive . . . that you must be frustrated forever. You *can* have victory in your life when you realize this principle: *God will never tell you to do something without giving you the power to do it!* God's Word says, "Be kind and compassionate to one another, forgiving each other, just as in Christ God forgave you" (Ephesians 4:32). When you have received Jesus Christ as your personal Lord and Savior, giving Him control of your life, you have residing within you the presence and power of the almighty God. God's word also says, "The one who calls you is faithful and he will do it" (1 Thessalonians 5:24).

Certainly, the Lord has felt your pain of rejection: "He was despised and rejected by men, a man of sorrows, and familiar with suffering" (Isaiah 53:3). Yet while still on the cross, Jesus made the choice to forgive those who were mocking and crucifying Him. He prayed, "Father, forgive them, for they do not know what they are doing" (Luke 23:34). Now with Christ's life within you, you too can forgive—in His power, in His strength. Claim this assurance: "I can do everything through him who gives me strength" (Philippians 4:13).

As you seek to deal with your painful past, I pray that the following steps will be of great help to you.

Confess the Hurt (Face the Offense)

Forgiveness does not deny or minimize the hurt caused or the harm done.

When Jesus appeared to the disciples after His resurrection, He told doubting Thomas, "Put your finger here; see my hands. Reach out your hand and put it into my side" (John 20:27). Jesus still bore the scars of the pain and suffering of His crucifixion. He showed that He did not need to deny or minimize His pain and suffering in order to forgive.

He will probably bear the scars for all eternity. Likewise, you do not need to "change the truth" of your painful past.

Choose to Heal (Forgive Your Parents)

Forgiveness is undeserved.

If you think that those who hurt you don't *deserve* forgiveness you're right! Forgiveness is based not on justice, but on grace (giving someone a gift that is not deserved). You *choose* to bestow undeserved grace and mercy on the offender . . . just like the grace and mercy Christ chose to bestow on you by offering you salvation. As Ephesians 2:8,9 says: "For it is by grace you have been saved, through faith—and this not from yourselves, it is the gift of God—not by works, so that no one can boast." Therefore, your forgiveness will be based not on another person's change of heart, but on the choice from your heart to give grace and mercy.

Forgiveness is not a feeling; it's a choice of obedience to God's command.

"Bear with each other and forgive whatever grievances you may have against one another. Forgive as the Lord forgave you" (Colossians 3:13). You don't have to *feel* like forgiving to forgive. Forgiveness is a conscious act of the will to release the right to retribution and revenge—to release the right to resentment. Surely Stephen, while being stoned, did not feel like forgiving his attackers, yet he made a choice to forgive, praying: "Lord, do not hold this sin against them" (Acts 7:60).

Choosing to forgive doesn't mean your feelings will automatically change or that your heart is instantly healed. The healing of a broken arm doesn't occur overnight; likewise, the healing of a broken heart may take considerable time. That is normal. Remember, you don't have to *feel* forgiving in order to forgive. Ultimately, forgiveness is a choice to obey God.

Forgiveness does not mean forgetting.

Perhaps you've heard the phrase "forgive and forget" and said, "Impossible!" When you choose to forgive someone, that does not mean you get a case of "holy amnesia." God doesn't have amnesia either. When you read that He chooses to remember your sins no more that simply means that He will not hold your sins against you anymore. Consider: It takes far more character to remember wrongs and forgive them, than to deny wrongs as though they never happened. It is the remembering of wrongs that makes extending forgiveness necessary.

Come to Harmony (Free Yourself)

Forgiveness is your path to freedom.

Have you said, "I've tried to forgive, but it doesn't work"? Understand that forgiveness is not usually a one-time act, but rather *a process* of forgiving again and again. In Matthew 18:21,22 we see that forgiveness is not based on the other person's response either: "Peter came to Jesus and asked, 'Lord, how many times shall I forgive my brother when he sins against me? Up to seven times?' Jesus answered, 'I tell you, not seven times, but seventy-seven times.' " The verbal interaction of someone asking for forgiveness and the verbal granting of that request may be comforting; however, such interaction is not essential for true forgiveness. Even when your offender is deceased, you can still forgive because forgiveness is an act within your heart alone. In fact, forgiveness is possible for anyone for anything at any time, "for nothing is impossible with God" (Luke 1:37).

Forgiveness does not let the offender "off the hook."

When you forgive, you are not freeing the offender from facing the consequences of wrongdoing. Your sovereign God, who sees all and knows all, also knows how to deal with the offender in the way that will be most poignantly felt. The Lord says, "It is mine to avenge; I will repay" (Romans 12:19).

Forgiveness is reinforced with prayer.

> *Lord, I acknowledge the pain from my past. . . . I was deeply hurt. Although I hate what happened, I refuse to harbor hatred in my heart, for I know unforgiveness will only keep me in bondage to bitterness. Because You have freely forgiven me for choosing wrong, I am now choosing to forgive those who have wronged me. I will no longer be their judge. I release them into Your sovereign care, for I know You judge justly. Now, because the Prince of Peace lives within me, I claim the peace You have promised me. Thank You for setting me free.*

Precious child of God, settle past accounts God's way. Only then will you receive the peace He promises. Even if, at times, it seems too hard to forgive, take His Word to heart: "You need to persevere so that when you have done the will of God, you will receive what he has promised" (Hebrews 10:36).

30

God's Will

Hitting the Target

Dear June,

Just before my grandfather died, he said he had missed God's call on his life. I don't want this to happen to me—how do I find God's will? I don't want to waste my life and end up like my grandfather. Instead, I want to count for God. I'm seeking to find the center of His will, but I don't know what that is.

Dear Target Seeker,

How God will honor your heart so yielded to Him! You may find it helpful to know that God's will doesn't really have a "center." It is not a tiny, hard-to-hit target that requires great expertise to hit! His will is much bigger and broader than you imagine. God's will is His ideal plan, His good and perfect intention, which He wants you to know more than anything. So why is there such difficulty?

God's Permanent Will

Much of God's will is crystal clear as presented through biblical principles—such as "keep the Ten Commandments" (Exodus 20) and "stay sexually pure" (1 Thessalonians 4). These biblical principles are *God's permanent will* and apply to *every* believer. If you are sincerely living in concert with the truths from God's Word, then take heart—you are *already* walking in God's will.

God's Personalized Will

What you seem to be searching for is *God's personalized will,* which is unique to every believer. While you can know God's permanent will by knowing God's Word, you cannot know God's personalized will without God's guidance. For example, the Bible tells us all to "serve God" (Deuteronomy 10:20)—that is His permanent will—but the Bible is not explicit about *how* you should do this. You could serve God by singing in the choir, teaching a Bible class, serving on church committees, feeding the hungry, reaching the needy, nurturing children, counseling teens, and so on—but you can't do it all! The Lord alone is able to reveal what is right for you personally. He stands ready to give you the right role for the right activity at the right time in the right place! Finding His personalized will means discerning not just the good from the bad, but also the best from the better. So, *God's permanent will is written in the Bible,* whereas *God's personalized will is written on your heart.*

Growth with God

If you really want to know the will of God the Father—both His *permanent* and *personalized* will—your primary priority must be to grow deeper in an intimate relationship with God the Son. With full imagery, Jesus describes this vital and vibrant relationship: "I am the vine; you are the branches. If a man remains in me and I in him, he will bear much fruit; apart from me you can do nothing" (John 15:5).

To illustrate this truth, assume that at age seven you are adopted by a young, childless couple. When you first enter their home, you have no idea what "their will" is for you. You have no clue as to what bedroom to use or what freedoms or restrictions you have. Since you've not known your new parents long, you can't know their will. Only after you spend *time* with them, seeking to understand their hearts, will you sense their will for you. Likewise, the closer you are to Christ, the clearer His will is to you.

In God's eyes your *relationship with Him* is far more important than any role you play for Him. He wants *intimacy* with you more than He wants your busy-work activities! His emphasis on having a love relationship with you is summed up in Matthew 22:37, "Love the Lord your God with all your heart and with all your soul and with all your mind."

Your life will find fulfillment not in a regimen of rules, but in a relationship with Christ. So why go through the regimen of reading the Bible? Because the more you read God's Word, the more you know God's thoughts; and the more you know God's thoughts, the more you know God's will. Romans 12:2 presents this growth challenge, "Do not conform any longer to the pattern of this world, but be transformed by the renewing of your mind. Then you will be able to test and approve what God's will is—his good, pleasing and perfect will."

Guidance From God

God is not playing a game of "hide and seek" to make finding His will fun for Him and frustrating for you. In fact, God has promised to guide you through every decision in your life. In Psalm 32:8 the Lord assures you of His active involvement: "I will instruct you and teach you in the way you should go; I will counsel you and watch over you." Practically speaking, how does God give you His special, supernatural guidance?

God's Guiding Hand

God Guides You Through . . .		*You Follow God's Guidance by . . . .*
Gifts	(Romans 12:4-8)	Reflecting on your God-given abilities
Understanding	(Proverbs 24:32)	Using your common sense and practical reasoning
Impressions	(John 16:13)	Becoming sensitive to the prompting of the Holy Spirit
Desires	(Philippians 2:13)	Knowing that God places His own desires into your heart
Advice	(Proverbs 15:22)	Seeking counsel from wise and godly people
Necessities	(1 Timothy 5:8)	Prioritizing the primary responsibilities in your life

Circumstances	(John 5:19,20)	Getting involved where you see God is at work
Enlightenment	(Ephesians 1:17,18)	Praying for wisdom and to know Christ better

Look up and meditate on each Scripture above for deeper insights.

As you seek to know God's will, what about your concerns the Bible does not address? Do you "just do the best that you can?" No! To reveal God's personalized will, the Spirit of Christ is in you right now as *your personal Counselor!* Ephesians 1:13 and 14 say that when you received Jesus Christ as your Savior, you received the Holy Spirit to reside within your human spirit—permanently. In John 16:13, Jesus said that the Spirit of Truth "will guide you into all truth . . . and he will tell you what is yet to come." Christ's Spirit in you will *teach* your mind how to think, *direct* your will how to act, and *affect* your emotions to feel in all the ways that are right in God's sight.

The next time you seek God's will, consider God's whole "target range" of possibilities by asking yourself these three questions:

- Has God spoken specifically about this in His Holy Word? *If so, do it!*
- Am I saying or doing anything that misses the mark of what is right in God's sight? *If so, change it!*

- Have I earnestly prayed for the Spirit of Christ to reveal His will to me? *If not, pray it!*

If prayer is hard for you, you can get started by saying:

Heavenly Father, I sincerely need Your wisdom to know Your will. Thank You for giving me Your Holy Spirit to guide me into all truth and for the Savior who is my source of strength to stay in Your will. I now yield my will to Your will.

I desire to do your will, O my God; your law is within my heart (Psalm 40:8).

31

Salvation

What About the Upardonable Sin?

Dear June,

I've had a rebellious and defiant attitude toward God and His Word, and I've said and thought things I wish I hadn't. My problem is that I'm afraid I've committed the unpardonable sin spoken of in Mark 3:28,29. Please tell me exactly what this means and whether I can still be forgiven. I want to be saved, but I'm afraid I've blown it.

Dear Afraid,

I'm glad you feel the freedom to share your concern over your salvation and whether you have committed the unpardonable sin. Please know you are not alone; many others suffer agonizing fear because of confusion over what sin Jesus is referring to in Mark 3:29: "But whoever blasphemes against the Holy Spirit will never be forgiven; he is guilty of eternal sin." The very fact that you care, that you have a repentant heart, and that salvation is important to you shows that God is working in your life in a very meaningful way.

In your letter you referred to three important spiritual terms which are interrelated. They are *salvation, forgiveness,* and *rebellion*. I would like to respond briefly to each term before we examine the passage in Mark which mentions the unforgivable sin.

Salvation

Your last sentence states, "I want to be saved, but I'm afraid I've blown it." Just in case you may not be aware, the "doctrine of eternal security" means that authentic Christians permanently possess eternal life, that salvation is a gift, and all you have to do is receive it. This gift was initiated by God the Father, accomplished through God the Son, and is guaranteed by God the Holy Spirit. (See Ephesians 1:4,13,14,7 respectively.) You have the assurance that you possess this wonderful gift—a gift which God has promised you will never lose (John 10:28)—if you have:

Confessed your sin (1 John 1:9)

- Agreed with God that you are a sinner
- Agreed with God that the payment for sin is death

Repented of your sin (Acts 3:19)

- Changed your mind about sin
- Changed your direction away from sin

Believed Jesus Christ paid the penalty for your sin (John 3:16)

- Realized that your salvation rests in Jesus Christ alone
- Realized that you cannot earn your own salvation by being good

Received Jesus Christ as your Lord (Colossians 2:6)

- Lived in the awareness that the Spirit of Christ is in you
- Lived in submission to Christ by growing in His likeness

Forgiveness

God's forgiveness seems too good to be true, but it is a natural companion of salvation. His gift of eternal life and His promise to forgive all your sins (past, present, and future) walk together hand in hand. Unfortunately, many Christians who have experienced an absence of love and forgiveness from the significant people in their lives have real difficulty believing that God is waiting with open arms when they acknowledge their sins and failures. If you are concerned that your rebellious and defiant heart has taken you beyond God's forgiveness, then confess and forsake your past. Go to God with a sincere desire to live in a way that pleases Him. "If we confess our sins, he is faithful and just and will forgive us our sins and purify us from all unrighteousness" (1 John 1:9). To reinforce the truth of God's forgiveness, look up and memorize the following Scriptures:

2 Chronicles 7:14	Proverbs 28:13
Psalm 32:5	Jeremiah 31:34
Psalm 86:5	Ephesians 1:7
Psalm 103:12	Hebrews 8:12

Rebellion

Mârâh, the Old Testament Hebrew word meaning "to rebel," signified an opposition to authority which was motivated by pride. This word was generally used throughout Scripture to indicate a disobedient attitude toward God. Interestingly, the Old Testament historical account which relates the rebellious condition of the nation Israel is a biblical pageant of the contentious nature we are all born with! Briefly, Israel was in bondage to the Egyptians (a picture of our slavery to sin). God delivered them (salvation), then set them on course to the Promised Land. In the beginning they worshiped and obeyed God with thankful hearts, but as life became difficult, complaints, bitterness, and outright rebellion prevailed. God allowed Israel to experience the consequences of their actions (see Jeremiah 4:16–18 for an example) because of their disobedience. But God loved them and had compassion for them and forgave their sins of rebellion (see Lamentations 3:31,32 and Jeremiah 33:8).

✔It is important to realize that anyone who is violating the revealed will of God is rebellious. Rebellion can reside in the heart of anyone at any age, "for all have sinned and fall short of the glory of God" (Romans 3:23). Yet God continues to seek the heart and speak to the heart, "I have swept away your offenses like a cloud, your sins like the morning mist. Return to me, for I have redeemed you" (Isaiah 44:22).

The Unpardonable Sin

Now, let's examine the passage of Scripture you mentioned in the Gospel of Mark. The Amplified Bible gives more detail than some other versions. Mark 3:28,29 reads:

> Truly and solemnly I say to you, all sins will be forgiven the sons of men, and whatever abusive and blasphemous things they utter; but whoever speaks abusively against or maliciously misrepresents the Holy Spirit can never get forgiveness, but is guilty of and is in the grasp of an everlasting trespass.

Although these two verses by themselves seem to say that speaking against the Holy Spirit is the unpardonable sin, looking at them in the context of verses 22–30 (AMP) will give you a broader perspective. Let's focus on verse 22.

The phrase "abusively and maliciously misrepresenting the Holy Spirit" is in fact a hardened-heart attitude. In verse 22, the scribes were rejecting the Holy Spirit and attributing His work to Satan. Their sin was refusing the saving grace of Jesus Christ and the Holy Spirit, the very hand by which salvation comes.

One of the functions of the Holy Spirit is to draw people to Christ—to exalt Christ. Another function of the Holy Spirit is to convict people of their sinful state and of their subsequent need of a savior. The only unpardonable sin is the unwillingness to yield to the convicting work of the Holy Spirit which leads to salvation through Jesus Christ. Blasphemy against the Holy Spirit is a complete and total hardening of the heart to the extent that the convicting work of the Holy Spirit is completely rejected and even attributed to Satan. It is not that God does not have the power to forgive this sin; it is that the person completely, repeatedly, and totally rejects the offer of forgiveness and reconciliation to God.

To further illustrate this truth, let me give this analogy. Once there was a man who was caught up in a flooding river while in his fishing boat. Being a God-fearing man, he began to pray for deliverance. As his boat neared a populated area along the river, some townspeople quickly set about to rescue him by throwing ropes to him from the riverbank. Others boarded large heavy boats with powerful engines capable of maneuvering with ease through the forceful waters of the river. The man, ignoring the ropes and rescue boats, yelled out to the people that they were not godly people and that their attempts to help him were not of God but of the devil. Therefore, he continued to be swept downriver all the while praying fervently to God to save him. Soon the man heard the sound of a helicopter overhead and, looking up, saw a ladder being lowered to his boat for him to climb up to safety. Once again he ignored the means by which his salvation was offered. He yelled to the rescuers that they were not of God and that their attempts to save him were of Satan. The man continued praying to God for help up to the time he and his small fishing craft plunged headlong over Niagara Falls—falling to their destruction on the perilous rocks below. As the man stood before God, he demanded to know why God refused to heed his cries and save him. God responded by rebuking the man, telling him that He had indeed heard and responded to his cries for help. First He sent the townspeople and then the helicopter to save him. But the man refused to accept the hands God offered to save his life and consequently lost his life. In the same way, you cannot be saved if you reject the Holy Spirit, the very hand by which salvation comes!

Since the Holy Spirit is apparently working in your life and drawing you to Christ, you have obviously not committed the "unpardonable" sin.

The Lord Jesus Christ could be knocking on your heart's door right now, waiting for you to open the door for Him to come in.

Do you recognize your need to be saved? If you are willing to confess and repent of your sin, believe that Jesus Christ died in your place for you sin and are ready to receive Him as your Lord and Savior, you can pray this prayer right now.

> Lord Jesus, I have lived much of my life my way. I didn't really care about living life Your way. My rebellion has pushed me even further away. Please forgive me for my prideful sin. I'm asking You, the Lord Jesus Christ, to come into my heart to take control of my life. Thank You for saving me. Please make me the kind of person You want me to be. Amen.

[Jesus said,] "Whoever wants to save his life will lose it, but whoever loses his life for me will find it" (Matthew 16:25).

32

Self-Worth

Seeing Yourself Through God's Eyes

Dear June,

I have a real hard time believing that the Lord loves me. I know He loves everyone, but somehow I don't fit into that category. I must have the worst inferiority complex there ever was. How can I get my mind off myself and this dilemma so I can love others?

Dear Loved One,

It would bring me great joy for you to come to know how much God loves you. Your need for unconditional love is a God-given desire: "What a man desires is unfailing love" (Proverbs 19:22a). He planted that need in order to turn your desires toward Him. God knows that people fail people; only He has an "unfailing love for you" (Isaiah 54:10). So even if you don't feel it, believe it!

Often we confuse *eros,* the emotional, valentine kind of love, for *agape,* which is the Greek word used in the

New Testament for God's love. *Agape* love is not "here today—gone tomorrow"; rather it is a commitment to seek another's highest good no matter what he or she does or doesn't do. Consequently, when you read that "God is love" (1 John 4:8), understand that God has a commitment to seek your highest good—no matter what!

See Yourself Through God's Eyes

It is one thing to *know* about God's love, but quite another thing to *feel* it and incorporate it into your life. Knowing that, God has provided some ways to help you move the knowledge of His love from your head to your heart where you can feel it and be comforted and motivated by it.

Discover your true worth. Your worth is not based on the opinions of others or how well you perform before others. It is not measured by being accepted or rejected by others. How do you determine worth? If you were to take an item to an auction, its worth would be established based on the highest price paid. So what are you worth? Jesus Christ paid the ultimate price for you when He came to earth as a man, willingly died on the cross, and paid the penalty for your sins. He loved you enough to die for you (see 1 John 3:16; 4:9,10). And that's not all! If you have truly yielded your will to His will to become an authentic Christian, He sees you as "holy in his sight, without blemish and free from accusation" (Colossians 1:22).

Decide to depend on the everlasting and never-changing truth of God's love. "We know and rely on the love God has for us" (1 John 4:16). He knows your heart because He created you in your innermost being, as the psalmist said, "You are familiar with all my ways" (Psalm 139:3). No human being could ever know you like God knows you, yet He is the one who loves you most dearly. In light of these truths, I encourage you to say, "Thank You, Lord, that Your love for me is everlasting. Thank You that I can always rely on Your love."

Develop new thought patterns by personalizing Scripture which speaks to you of God's love for you. A good place to begin is by adapting 1 Corinthians 13:4–8: "God is patient with me" or "God keeps no records of my wrongs." A wonderful psalm which has powerfully changed the lives of many Christians is Psalm 139. I urge you to personalize this psalm, write it out, and commit it to memory. Repeat it over and over again until the truths it contains permeate the very core of your being and become *your reality.*

Draw near to God with your true feelings and fears. James 4:8 says, "Come near to God and he will come near to you." Be willing to look at the hurts and rejections from your past, then allow God's soothing touch to heal those tender and sensitive wounds of your heart.

Determine that you will live out your desire to reach out and love others. "Since God so loved us, we also ought to love one another" (1 John 4:11). With your mind off yourself and on Christ, you will naturally seek to meet the needs of others. Encouraging someone else actually builds your own sense of value and worth.

Depend on your identity in Christ when you don't feel worthy. If you have accepted Jesus as your Lord and Savior, then you have a new identity. "Therefore, if anyone is in

Christ, he is a new creation; the old has gone, the new has come!" (2 Corinthians 5:17). When God looks at you, He sees His Son. Read Ephesians 3:14–20 and begin to realize these truths:

- You have Christ in you.
- You are rooted in love.
- You have the power to grasp the depth of this love.
- You *can* know this love.

Steps to Self-Acceptance

Many reasons underlie the fact that we all, at one time or another, have had difficulty accepting God's love. Who has not experienced criticism and discouraging remarks from people important to us! As children we desperately reached for the love and approval of others. Yet we found ourselves empty. As teenagers we were caught by the deadly "trap of comparisons"—comparing ourselves with others and falling short. Now as adults, we must put away these childish things. "When I was a child, I talked like a child, I thought like a child, I reasoned like a child. When I became a man, I put childish ways behind me" (1 Corinthians 13:11). Because you are now an adult, you must—

- *Accept* that you will not be liked or loved by everyone. In fact, no one is liked by everyone! Jesus said, "If the world hates you, keep in mind that it hated me first. . . . If they persecuted me, they will persecute you also . . ." (John 15:18,20). So, accept that some people whom you like will not like you in return.

Accept yourself as acceptable to God. "Accept one another, then, just as Christ accepted you . . ." (Romans 15:7). You were accepted by God not because you did anything to deserve or earn it. He chose to accept you because He loves you.

Accept that you will make mistakes. You are not perfect. No one is. Don't condemn yourself when you fail. The Lord knew you would fail before you were born. Yet He still chose to accept you. Even the apostle Paul said, "Not that I have already obtained all this, or have already been made perfect, but I press on to take hold of that for which Christ Jesus took hold of me. Brothers, I do not consider myself yet to have taken hold of it. But one thing I do: Forgetting what is behind and straining toward what is ahead, I press on toward the goal to win the prize for which God has called me heavenward in Christ Jesus" (Philippians 3:12–14).

Accept criticism and the responsibility for failure. When you fail don't make excuses. Don't try to make yourself look better or justify any wrong attitude or actions. Say, "I was wrong and I take full responsibility. Will you please forgive me?" "Before his downfall a man's heart is proud, but humility comes before honor" (Proverbs 18:12).

Accept God as the only one whom you are to please. Don't live for the approval of anyone except the Lord. If He is your highest priority, then you will be able to say *no* when you are being pressured to say *yes*. . . . You will be Spirit-led, not people-pressured. Let Galatians 1:10 be your test. "Am I now trying to win the approval of men, or of God? Or am I trying to please men? If I were still trying to please men, I would not be a servant of Christ" (Galatians 1:10).

Accept what you cannot change. Don't try to force people to be different or situations to be changed. Accept the Lord's loving watch and care over your life and live in total dependence on Him. Look to the Lord to be your Need-Meeter. "If any of you lacks wisdom, he should ask God, who gives generously to all without finding fault, and it will be given to him. But when he asks, he must believe and not doubt, because he who doubts is like a wave of the sea, blown and tossed by the wind" (James 1:5,6).

My friend, relax in God's love. Let Him love you. Let His love permeate your heart. After all, you are a child of the King. Bask in that truth!

How great is the love the Father has lavished on us, that we should be called children of God! . . . (1 John 3:1).

Part 8

Readiness to Reach Out

33

Caregiving

AIDING THE AGING

Dear June,

My mother passed away five years ago and now my dad is experiencing many health problems. After surviving two heart attacks, a broken hip, and eye surgery, a once healthy, active man is now very frail and uses a walker. He doesn't hear or see well and is almost a shut-in. Please help me with some suggestions on how I can be a loving daughter to him even though I work and have a family of my own.

Dear Caring Daughter,

The love and concern you have for your father is apparent in your warm letter. It seems you have entered that specific time in life that most of us have or will encounter, the time of the "sandwich generation." This term applies to us when we are squeezed between two generations whose needs demand all our time and resources.

Fortunately, God's love is spelled out in many different ways, and it doesn't require a lot of money or special training to meet the needs of your dad or any elderly or lonely "shut-in." The most important job requirement for someone who becomes a caregiver is a willing heart and helping hands.

Pray for a Willing Heart

The Son of Man did not come to be served, but to serve, and to give his life as a ransom for many (Matthew 20:28).

- *Pray* daily for your father.
- *Pray* that God will develop within you a servant's heart.
- *Pray* for God to provide windows of time to be with your dad.
- *Pray* for discernment to determine his specific needs.
- *Pray* for the wisdom to maintain priorities according to your God-given responsibilities.

Hints for Helping Hands

Each of you should look not only to your own interests, but also to the interests of others (Philippians 2:4).

- *Limit* your visits in the beginning to twenty or thirty minutes. Just sitting together outside, enjoying God's beautiful creation, greatly lifts the spirit.

- *Laugh* a lot. Tell funny stories from your daily experiences. No one ever outgrows the need for laughter. Proverbs 17:22 says, "A cheerful heart is good medicine, but a crushed spirit dries up the bones."

- *Lighten* a negative outlook by accentuating the positive. Look at the bright side of things and encourage him to do the same.

- *Love* him through words and touch. Tell him how special he is to you. Tell him again and again and again. Hug and kiss him whenever possible.

- *Listen* patiently to him—even to stories you've heard before. Ask questions that encourage him to talk about his life, experiences, and feelings.

- *Look* for things that are hard for him to do and do them (take out the trash, change light bulbs, pick up old newspapers, mow the lawn, clean out the refrigerator).

- *Let* the Holy Spirit reveal his spiritual needs. Share Christ with him if he does not know the Lord as his Savior. "But in your hearts set apart Christ as Lord. Always be prepared to give an answer to everyone who asks you to give the reason for the hope that you have. But do this with gentleness and respect" (1 Peter 3:15).

I cannot emphasize enough that God is just as concerned about you as He is for your father and his needs. If you have a sincere desire to help others, your tendency is probably to assume too much responsibility and overdo! Thus, as God's instrument of love and care in your father's life, you can easily become disappointed, depressed, and defeated. I encourage you to overcome your inclination to overdo by taking to heart these practical areas.

Don'ts of Caregiving

Don't do everything for your dad. *Read* Galatians 6:5.

- Encourage personal accountability.
- Give responsibilities to him whenever possible.

Don't think you have to know all the answers. *Read* Proverbs 18:12–13.

- Listen carefully for his hurts and feelings.
- Learn to respond in ways that express that you understand.

Don't try to control your father or his circumstances. *Read* Romans 8:9.

- Submit to the leading and control of the Holy Spirit.
- Recognize that God has purposes to accomplish in both of your lives.

Don't take things too seriously. *Read* Proverbs 17:22.

- Focus on the positives.
- Learn to laugh at little things.

Don't seek your identity in becoming a "need-meeter" to others. *Read* Colossians 3:3.

- Realize your true identity is in Christ.
- Know that God is the one who gives your life meaning and purpose.

Don't stuff your own feelings of hurt and frustration. *Read* Psalm 62:8.

- Pour out your heart to the Lord.
- Share your feelings with a trusted friend.

Don't become physically exhausted. *Read* Mark 6:31,32.

- Set aside time to be alone.
- Maintain personal boundaries.

Don't become isolated from family and friends. *Read* Proverbs 27:9b.

- Keep in contact with others.
- Get time away on a regular basis.

Don't try to do it all alone. *Read* Numbers 11:16,17.

- Delegate others to help.
- Seek professional help.

Don't become spiritually depleted. *Read* Psalm 119:71.

- Thank God for the opportunity to serve the Lord by serving another.
- Let pressures become motivation to increase your time reading God's Word.

In closing, I would like to share answers to some questions you may have because of your elderly dad. I hope these will be helpful as you continue to be a representative of God's love to your father.

Questions and Answers on Caring for a Loved One

If my dad becomes difficult, can I keep from becoming bitter?

Choose to sincerely forgive, considering how much God has already forgiven you. "Bear with each other and forgive whatever grievances you may have against one another. Forgive as the Lord forgave you" (Colossians 3:13).

How can I handle the difficult time demands?

Develop a daily schedule, giving quality time to your dad. Remember, the past is gone and the future is unsure; today may be all you have. "If anyone does not provide for his relatives, and especially for his immediate family, he has denied the faith and is worse than an unbeliever" (1 Timothy 5:8).

What do I do if my dad becomes childish?

Recognize that the roles of parent and child often reverse in later life. Taking the responsibility for your elderly parent is putting your love into practice and is pleasing to God. "But if a widow has children or grandchildren, these should learn first of all to put their religion into practice by caring for their own family and so repaying their parents and grandparents, for this is pleasing to God" (1 Timothy 5:4).

What should I do when my dad experiences memory loss?

Remember, the elderly are weak and you are strong. Exhibit the same loving strength and patience that God has given you. "We who are strong ought to bear with the failings of the weak" (Romans 15:1).

How should I treat my dad when he becomes stubborn?

Apply the Golden Rule: "Do to others as you would have them do to you" (Luke 6:31).

How important is physical affection?

Everyone needs as much embracing, hugging, kissing, and touching as possible. "Greet one another with a kiss of love" (1 Peter 5:14).

Should I ever "force" my dad to leave his home?

Honor his desire to remain at home unless it becomes *absolutely necessary* to make other arrangements. " 'Honor your father and mother'—which is the first commandment with a promise—'that it may go well with you and that you may enjoy long life on the earth' " (Ephesians 6:2,3).

Should I direct the decision-making of my dad?

Show the same respect you would desire. Allow your father as much freedom as possible. "Show respect for the elderly" (Leviticus 19:32).

Let us not become weary in doing good, for at the proper time we will reap a harvest if we do not give up (Galatians 6:9).

34

Intimacy

TRAVELING TOGETHER

Dear June,

I feel as though I don't have a husband. Physically he deprives me of his closeness and emotionally our conversations are superficial. If I reach out, I find a "cold body" that doesn't give more than a few minutes to me and soon heads out to do something of his own. What he really would like to do is watch TV and have his old bachelor's life without any responsibilities at home. What can I do? How can our relationship be healed?

Dear Deprived,

Your longing for closeness with your husband is not only normal but also desirable. One of God's designs for marriage is growth in intimacy. Since you lack both emotional and physical closeness with your husband, you are wise in seeking the tools to pave the way to a more intimate relationship.

Intimacy involves two people who both feel secure enough to share their inmost beings. For you and your husband to walk together in oneness, you must both be in agreement. Amos 3:3 says, "Do two walk together unless they have agreed to do so?" But how do you arrive at that agreement?

Steps to Getting Started

Step 1: Pray that God will prepare your husband's heart and show you the right time to approach him.

Step 2: When there are no distractions and he is in a pleasant mood, tell him you would like to talk with him a few moments. Then ask, "Is now a good time?" If it's not, *let him* select the best time.

Step 3: When you do talk, ask several straightforward questions which can be answered with a simple *yes* or *no:*

- "Do you feel our marriage is all that it could be or should be?"
- "Do you sometimes wish we could understand each other better?"
- "Would you be willing for us to try a project to make our marriage more fulfilling?"

Step 4: Tell him this project is very important because you want to be the best mate possible for him. In order to accomplish that, you need to know what is most meaningful to him.

- "Could we agree to meet together once a week over the next four weeks for at least thirty minutes to learn to communicate better?"
- "I believe this investment of time will be like a financial investment for us which will pay large dividends in the future."

Step 5: Set a regular time and place for talking. State that if you both find these meetings helpful, you will continue, but that there is no obligation beyond the first four weeks. (This will "let him off the hook" and show that you are sensitive to his feelings.)

> The wise in heart are called discerning, and pleasant words promote instruction (Proverbs 16:21).

Strides Toward Sensitive Sharing

In the first meeting, set a goal to hear each other's feelings. The following "sentence starters" will move you down the path from surface talk to more intimate conversation. As you both complete each sentence, talk thoroughly about your answers before going on. (In the first session, don't be surprised if you cover only the first few sentences.)

- I feel your greatest character quality is . . .
- I feel my greatest asset is . . .
- If I could change one thing about the way I was raised it would be . . .
- Two things that make you easy to be with are . . .
- An important change I would like to see in myself is . . .
- An important change I would like to see in you is . . .
- The most fulfilling aspect of my work is . . .
- I am most concerned about . . .
- A personal goal of mine is . . .
- The three things I value most about our relationship are . . .
- It would please me greatly for you to become interested in . . .
- My three most earnest prayers are . . .

In the coming weeks you may want to make up your own sentence starters. Don't be legalistic about how many questions you answer or how much time you spend. Above all, don't be critical or negative. God can use your understanding heart to spark the same desire for intimacy within your husband!

> The purposes of a man's heart are deep waters, but a man of understanding draws them out (Proverbs 20:5).

Stumbling Blocks to Sidestep

If at any point your husband responds negatively, don't let that slow you down by groveling in false guilt. Remove the following stumbling blocks (or myths) and replace them with God's truth.

Myth 1: ***Intimacy is found only in a relationship with someone of the opposite sex.***

Truth: Just as Jesus had an intimate friendship with Lazarus (John 11:5,33–36), intimacy can be developed between family members, friends, coworkers, roommates, or any two people who share deeply.

Action: Pray for and nurture several meaningful relationships. Set aside quality time to ask questions and share on the feeling level—don't talk just about facts.

> *There is a friend who sticks closer than a brother* (Proverbs 18:24).

Myth 2: ***Intimacy is always expressed physically.***

Truth: Intimacy can be expressed emotionally, mentally, and spiritually, as well as physically.

Action: Involve yourself with the whole person by asking, "What is the most meaningful thing I could do or be for you?" Then seek to do or be it.

Honor one another above yourselves (Romans 12:10).

Myth 3: ***Intimacy is quickly developed.***

Truth: Intimacy is the result of a gradual growth process.

Action: To grow in intimacy, learn to speak the other person's language of love—preparing favorite foods, giving favorite gifts, prioritizing favorite people, helping with favorite hobbies.

Each of you should look not only to your own interests, but also to the interests of others (Philippians 2:4).

Myth 4: ***Marriage will produce intimacy naturally.***

Truth: In many marriages intimacy *never* develops.

Action: Don't live for your mate to change—he may not. You can learn to be content with less as you nurture your relationship with the Lord and other people.

I have learned the secret of being content in any and every situation. . . . I can do everything through him who gives me strength (Philippians 4:12,13).

Traveling down the road to intimacy is like traveling in a foreign country and trying to read road signs which are written in another language. *For your husband, intimacy is foreign . . . even intimidating!* It threatens his sense of security. He may have been so deeply wounded in the past that he now protects himself from becoming hurt again. The problem is that the walls he once built to protect himself may now imprison him.

Although it has been disheartening, don't feel devastated if your mate continues to refuse a more intimate marriage. After all, the most intimate relationship possible is the one you can have with Jesus. Realize that as a Christian, you have "Christ *in* you" (Colossians 1:27). With His indwelling presence, Jesus will be your most intimate friend and your traveling companion for life.

> *You have made known to me the path of life; you will fill me with joy in your presence . . .* (Psalm 16:11).

35

Reconciliation

Building Blocks of Restoration

Dear June,

My grown children have virtually turned their backs on me. I've done some foolish things by marrying three times and this has caused them to turn away. But now I've seen and confessed my wrong, and I would like to rebuild a relationship with them. Can you help me?

Dear Hurting Parent,

The longing to have a close and loving relationship with your children is a natural desire, and I assure you that it is not too late for reconciliation. Now is the time to begin building bridges of unity and love in areas where there have been pain and suffering.

I, too, have done things which I regret. But looking at the past is good only if you use the mistakes and failures as learning tools, stepping-stones, and building blocks toward a better future. Dwelling on past failures keeps you from moving forward and hinders your effectiveness for God in the lives of others. You can determine to have Paul's attitude, "One thing I do: Forgetting what is behind and straining toward what is ahead, I press on toward the goal to win the prize for which God has called me heavenward in Christ Jesus" (Philippians 3:13,14).

Remember, it takes time to rebuild or restore damaged relationships, but the end result will be worth the effort you expend. I hope the following suggestions will be helpful as you seek God's solutions for resolving conflicts and learn to trust His timing for restoring relationships with your children.

Building Blocks

Believe God can restore the years the locusts have eaten.

Our God is the God of redemption. He is able to bring life out of death, to turn ashes on a forest floor into fertile soil from which new life springs forth and new forests grow heavenward. Just as He is able to bring rich, luscious fruit from dried vines, He is more than able to restore life to dead relationships and cause them to bear the fruit of love, joy, and peace. "I will repay you for the years the locusts have eaten" (Joel 2:25).

Begin reaching out to your children.

You did not say whether you try to meet with your children on any kind of regular basis or whether your time with them is limited to family gatherings. If you don't have much contact with your children, you might seek ways to establish contact with them on a routine basis. Begin now to establish a pattern which they can grow to depend on. Sharing a little time with them on a regular basis will become a building block to reconciliation. "Each of you should look not only to your own interests but also to the interests of others" (Philippians 2:4).

Become sensitive to God's leading.

> The wise in heart are called discerning, and pleasant words promote instruction (Proverbs 16:21).

Do not try to do too much too soon. It will help to show an interest in whatever your children are doing. . . .

- Invite them to your home or out to dinner.
- Pick up little gifts for them when you see something that reminds you of them.
- Provide for a need in their lives.

The idea is to be consistent with your attention and your love. By expressing your love in ways which meet the needs of your children rather than your own you are communicating love on their terms. Your efforts will be best received by them when you allow *their* needs to dictate the ways you show your love. Loving them on their terms also demonstrates your sincerity and unselfish motives.

Bathe your children in prayer.

Ask God to bless each of your children and their families. Beseech the Lord on their behalf and pray for their salvation if they are not Christians. The most effective weapon in your spiritual arsenal is prayer.

- Pray for God's will to be done in their lives.
- Pray for their hearts to be sensitive to God.
- Pray for God to protect them from the schemes of Satan.
- Pray that they will be strengthened by the power of the Holy Spirit and come to know Christ in a deep and personal way. (See Ephesians 3:16–19 for a specific prayer.)

Build toward ***restored*** *relationships.*

R*ely on God's power instead of your own ability.*

The LORD is my strength and my shield; my heart trusts in him, and I am helped (Psalm 28:7).

- Lean on the Lord for empathy and understanding.
- Realize when you are weak He is strong.

E*xamine yourself for incorrect attitudes and then be willing to change.*

Anyone, then, who knows the good he ought to do and doesn't do it, sins (James 4:17).

- Do my actions demonstrate love?
- Do I exhibit meekness?
- Do I speak well of my children?
- Do I show deference?

- Do I have a forgiving spirit?
- Do I focus on eternal values?

***S**eek forgiveness and apologize to your children.*

If you have been trapped by what you said. . . . Go and humble yourself; press your plea with your neighbor (Proverbs 6:2,3).

- Admit your faults and weaknesses to your children.
- Ask your children to forgive you when you fail.

***T**rust God to give your children a heart of reconciliation.*

May the Lord direct your hearts into God's love and Christ's perseverance (2 Thessalonians 3:5).

- Realize you have no power to change your children.
- Realize God's timing will probably be much longer than you expect.

***O**bey the ground rules of communication.*

Do not let any unwholesome talk come out of your mouths, but only what is helpful for building others up according to their needs, that it may benefit those who listen (Ephesians 4:29).

- Verbalize your feelings.
- Listen without interrupting.
- Use words that build self-worth.
- Offer unconditional acceptance.

***R**eflect the character of Christ.*

You, however, are controlled not by the sinful nature but by the Spirit (Romans 8:9).

- Die to your rights.
- Die to self-defense.
- Die to self-reliance.

***E**ngage a mediator, if necessary.*

But if he will not listen, take one or two others along, so that "every matter may be established by the testimony of two or three witnesses" (Matthew 18:16).

- Seek a family member or friend to help your children understand your heart.
- Encourage your children to confide in a mature Christian.

***D**o not hold yourself responsible for the outcome.*

And we know that in all things God works for the good of those who love him, who have been called according to his purpose (Romans 8:28).

- Reconciliation will not always happen.
- God may have a higher purpose to accomplish.

As you seek reconciliation, be prepared for the possibility that you will initially be met with rejection or anger. Commit to the Lord ahead of time to always respond in a loving and understanding way. When you pray, ask God to help you hear your children's hearts when you may not understand or agree with what they say. Also pray that your children will be given eyes to see your genuine love for them regardless of what may have happened in the past. It may take them a while to respond . . . but genuine, sacrificial, and consistent love is difficult to resist.

36

Suicide

Silent Cry for a Shepherd

Dear June,

Do you have any material on suicide? What are the signs of people who are contemplating suicide and how can I help them? I minister to those who suffer so much—many who have been misunderstood and rejected. Can you help me help them?

Dear Helper,

May God bless your shepherd's heart for wanting to help those who are going astray. The part you play can be pivotal—like the shepherd who seeks to save the lamb who is lost on the mountain ledge.

Suicide *is* a matter of life and death. Encouraging a despondent person to seek professional help (both physically and mentally) is advisable and often necessary. Meanwhile, as a friend you can recognize the signs of suicide and point people toward the Lord who will be—if they will let Him—the true Shepherd of their souls.

Recognize the Signs

No one commits suicide on impulse, yet friends and family often think the loss of their loved one was the result of an isolated moment of despair. In reality, suicide typically occurs after a long process of destructive and deductive thinking. Those who lose hope finally conclude that death is the *only logical solution.* As you recognize the signs of suicide, you will see sheep who are straying from the fold and hear their silent cry for help.

Early Signs

Depression	Change in eating and sleeping habits
Boredom	Decline in work or school performance
Avoidance of family	Inability to concentrate or make decisions
Anxiety	Lack of interest in the future

Advanced Signs

Dejection	Physical problems and complaints
Apathy	Excessive absenteeism
Self-pity	Withdrawal from family and friends
Rapid mood swings	Neglect of personal appearance

Danger Signs

Despair (no hope)	Alcohol and other drug abuse
Isolation	Getting personal affairs in order
Suicidal threats	Giving away personal possessions
Engulfing guilt	Sudden change from despair to peace

Suicide is a desperate act that, for one without hope, appears to be the only way out. It seems to be the only way of escape from an intolerable situation, whether it be physical or mental illness, loss, isolation, abuse, or guilt.

Respond to the Sorrow

People assume that only "black sheep" want to take their lives. However, successful people with status can be suicidal also. So can "popular" people, if they've lost all hope for inner peace. Even Christians with the truth—God's truth—can want to end their lives. They think "the Truth" won't work for them—they've not been "good enough."

What does a suicidal person need above everything else? Not compassion or love or sincerity or truth. Many who have been given all of those have still ended their lives. Why? They were still void of *hope*—hope for inner peace, hope for meaning and purpose. Yet Ecclesiastes 9:4 says, "Anyone who is among the living has hope." Seek to share that *where there is life there is hope!*

***H**onestly confront*

- Take seriously all talk of death or suicide and listen very carefully.
- Ask, "How are you really feeling? What is causing your deeper pain?"
- Seek to find out how the hurt is being handled.
- Ask the direct question, "Are you thinking about suicide?"
- Express your concern, "I care about your heart and know that God has a purpose for your life right now."

Rescue those being led away to death; hold back those staggering toward slaughter (Proverbs 24:11).

***O**ffer Options*

- Acknowledge the fact that life is hard: "At times we are all faced with having to choose from several unpleasant possibilities."
- List possible options, then rank them by preference.
- Point out that the goal is to choose the least unpleasant option.
- Seek agreement that self-destruction is not an option.
- Remove all impulse weapons such as guns and poisons.

No temptation has seized you except what is common to man. And God is faithful; he will not let you be tempted beyond what you can bear. But when you are tempted, he will also provide a way out so that you can stand up under it (1 Corinthians 10:13).

***P**resent a contract*

- Build a relationship by showing that you care and want to help.
- Ask for a contract, "Will you promise that if you are considering harming yourself, you will call me—day or night—before doing anything?"
- Put the contract in writing and be sure to get a signature.
- Write out Jeremiah 29:11 on an index card for your friend to read each morning and night.
- Make a commitment to stay in regular contact.

Two are better than one, because they have a good return for their work (Ecclesiastes 4:9).

***E**nlist help*

- Don't allow yourself to be sworn to secrecy.
- Contact a suicide crisis center.
- Arrange an appointment for your friend to get a physical checkup.
- Seek a trained counselor or therapist.
- Call a caring minister or youth director.

Plans fail for lack of counsel, but with many advisers they succeed (Proverbs 15:22).

Pray for the Holy Spirit to protect the person's mind from error. Explain to your friend, "The lie you are tempted to believe is that life has become impossible. The truth is, *with God all things are possible.*" (See Matthew 19:26.) When responding to needs, remember the most important action you can take is to point the downcast person to Christ Himself, the Shepherd of Hope for the hopeless.

Recommend the Shepherd

When a ram is crossing a stream, if its wool becomes saturated with water and the top-heavy sheep topples over, the animal is said to be "cast down." Without the aid of a shepherd, the sheep cannot stand up and will die.

In the Bible, God refers to people as sheep. Isaiah 53:6 accurately says, "We all, like sheep, have gone astray, each of us has turned to his own way." We all know we've gone astray and at times have even been cast down, unable to lift ourselves up. We have had to learn the painful lesson that we, too, could not save ourselves. That is why God the Father provided God the Son, as both our Savior and our Shepherd.

Because of the excess weight of their burdens, many people in life are thrown off balance and become emotionally downcast. Even the psalmist experienced such overwhelming sorrow that three different times he cried out, "Why are you downcast, O my soul? Why so disturbed within me?" Then three times he stated the solution for his own depression, "Put your hope in God, for I will yet praise him, my Savior and my God" (Psalm 42:5,11; 43:5).

Downcast sheep need to know that they are not unique—others have had the same difficulty. And they have received the help and hope that your friend, too, can receive.

Review the Reasoning

Downcast sheep must hear the truth—the truth that they have hope. Everyone needs to know the hope of God's purpose and peace. (God would not have created them if they did not have purpose.) But they also need to hear the reasons *not* to end their lives. They must hear how others would suffer if they destroyed their own lives. Thus, they need to see suicide as the most supremely selfish act—a defiant act in which they are assuming the role of God. As Jesus said to His wayward flock, "You will know the truth, and the truth will set you free" (John 8:32). *Compassionately* share these reasons to reject suicide and ask the despondent person to read out loud each of the Scriptures referenced.

- Suicide rejects God's offer of peace (Philippians 4:6,7).
- Suicide rejects God's plan for your life (Jeremiah 29:11).
- Suicide rejects God's design for your life (Psalm 139:13–16).
- Suicide rejects God's sovereignty over your life (Job 14:5).
- Suicide rejects God's ability to heal your hurts (Psalm 34:18).

- Suicide rejects God's right to guide you (Proverbs 3:5,6).
- Suicide rejects God's commandment not to kill (Exodus 20:13).
- Suicide rejects God's role as your Shepherd (Psalm 23).

Your care for the sheep who have gone astray will be a life-giving ministry. Sharing the Savior—His hope and His truth—is the *only logical solution*. The heavenly shepherd *can* save the "cast down"—He alone is the shepherd of their souls. "I am the good shepherd. The good shepherd lays down his life for his sheep" (John 10:11).

A Prayer for Beginning Again

Lord Jesus,

Life seems so difficult. . . . I need You as my Savior to save me from myself. Please forgive me for my sin—I want to begin again. Although I have strayed, be my Shepherd and guide me day by day. Because of Your forgiveness, I can now forgive others and even forgive myself. I accept my life even with its sorrows, and I trust You with my questions and with all of my tomorrows.

In Your precious name I pray,
Amen

37

Unbelieving Loved One

GIVING THE GREATEST GIFT

Dear June,

How can I witness to my mother when she doesn't believe in the Bible and is so fearful of true religion? Please help me. I love my family; I am firm in my God. My mother is just as firm against my views. We are being torn apart.

Dear Torn,

Because you are God's precious child, your heartache over your family conflict is of utmost importance to God. He shares your concern and knows the pain you are feeling over your mother's spiritual condition. He longs for her salvation more than you can possibly know.

Certainly God desires that your family know Him personally. Nevertheless, God always gives each person a choice whether or not to yield to Him. We cannot make that choice for others, no matter how much we love them and want what is best for them. As you seek to minister to your mother, I pray that you will take to heart the following thoughts.

Realize that your joy and fulfillment are not dependent upon your mother.

Every individual has been created with the need for unconditional love, significance, and security. It has been said that inside every person is a God-shaped vacuum that only He can fill. *Your needs are designed to draw you to God*—the only one who can truly meet your needs and fill the emptiness inside. This does not mean that you don't need people or that people don't meet some of your needs. Real joy comes as you learn to let go of the expectation that people will meet your needs and as you trust your only true Need-Neeter—Jesus Christ. What is God's promise in Philippians 4:19? "My God will meet all your needs according to his glorious riches in Christ Jesus."

Wage war for your mother in prayer.

Often people downplay the importance of prayer with statements like, "All I can do is pray." *Prayer is the most effective weapon in your spiritual arsenal.* James 5:16 says: "The prayer of a righteous man is powerful and effective." Scripture teaches that you are to be persistent in prayer. Ask and keep on asking, seek and keep on seeking, knock and keep on knocking. Matthew 7:7–11 says:

> Ask and it will be given to you; seek and you will find; knock and the door will be opened to

> you. For everyone who asks receives; he who seeks finds; and to him who knocks, the door will be opened. Which of you, if his son asks for bread, will give him a stone? Or if he asks for a fish, will give him a snake? If you, then, though you are evil, know how to give good gifts to your children, how much more will your Father in heaven give good gifts to those who ask him!

So pray for your mother:

Lord, use whatever circumstances necessary for Mother to open her heart to you. I pray she would come to the end of trying to meet her needs in her own power. May she see her spiritual need for Jesus Christ to be her Savior.

Continue to choose to love your mother.

The best thing you can do is be an example of God's love to her. In gentleness and quietness let God show Himself through you to her. Just as pictures often communicate more effectively than words, your loving behavior will speak far more powerfully than your words alone.

People who actively reject biblical truth usually do so out of fear and need. They tightly cling to what they feel brings them significance and security out of a fear that, if they let go, these needs will not be satisfied. Proverbs 19:22 reveals, "What a man desires is unfailing love." Therefore, I encourage you to ask God to show you ways in which you can actively demonstrate His love to your mother.

> Do you know your mother's language of love? How can you speak love to her . . . in gifts, in food, in the way time is spent? For example, I don't care about flowers, but I love puzzles and practical gifts. My mother doesn't care for Chinese food, but loves Mexican food so I often have cheese enchiladas for her because that's using her language of love. Make your list, then ask her for specifics. You may be surprised at some of her responses.

Finally, put "hands and feet" to your love—praying all the while that she would see Jesus in you.

Be prepared to defend your beliefs.

In 1 Peter 3:15,16, believers are told to "always be prepared to give an answer to everyone who asks you to give the reason for the hope that you have. But do this with gentleness and respect." You cannot change your mother's mind or heart, but you can respectfully respond with biblical truth. Though she presently may not believe the Bible, the Holy Spirit can use it to convict her of her need for the Savior and draw her to Himself. Hebrews 4:12 says: "The word of God is living and active. Sharper than any double-edged sword, it penetrates even to dividing soul and spirit, joints and marrow; it judges the thoughts and attitudes of the heart."

May I suggest that you have a warm, honest talk with your mother? Begin this way, "Mother, I really do care about what you think and feel. I want to hear your heart. Would you be willing to share with me some of the specific things that have given you a problem with believing the Bible?" Listen to her and write down all her points without interrupting her or being upset with her. Tell her you would like time to think seriously about her concerns. Then, after seeking out wise answers, share your responses with sensitivity and humility.

Let me illustrate this from my own life.

> A few months ago, my college-age niece said she couldn't believe the Bible any longer because her teacher had presented so many Bible "contradictions." For example, this teacher said that the Bible gave two different accounts of the creation which "proved" a contradiction. I said, "Oh, yes, there are two creation accounts, but they are not in conflict. In the first chapter of Genesis the universal creation is described much like a painting with a large brushstroke. Then the second chapter of Genesis fills in the picture, detailing the specific creation of man and woman. The former is an overview, the latter is a microscopic view of the whole." I've told my niece that every time she has a question to call me or write to me. If I don't know the answer, I will seek to find the answer, for God is not a God of contradictions. I also gave her three books on apologetics so she could learn how to answer the tough questions for herself. Today her faith is stronger than ever.

Major on the majors.

I also encourage you to keep your focus on the major truths of the Bible, and do not allow Satan to sidetrack you with controversies that will not matter that much in light of eternity. No matter what is brought up, never argue. Titus 3:9 says: "Avoid foolish controversies and genealogies and arguments and quarrels about the law, because these are unprofitable and useless."

Keep in mind that the Lord loves you and your mother more than you can ever comprehend. He has not stopped working in either of your lives. Isaiah 40:28 says: "He will not grow tired or weary, and his understanding no one can fathom." He understands more than you could ever know, and He sees the end from the beginning. In the midst of your concerns do not give up. Remember that God has not called you to save your mother but to love and honor her. Stand firm and trust the Lord with the results.

Subject Index

O

P

R

S

T

U

V

W

Topical Index of Scriptures

Abortion

Exodus 21:22,23
Deuteronomy 30:19
1 Samuel 12:23
Psalm 139:13,15,16
Proverbs 14:12; 24:11,12
Jeremiah 1:5; 29:11–14
John 9:1–3
1 Peter 3:15

Adultery

Genesis 50:20
Deuteronomy 32:4
1 Samuel 12:23
Psalm 141:3
Proverbs 10:12; 17:9
Ecclesiastes 3:7
Matthew 5:44
Acts 20:35
Romans 8:38,39
1 Corinthians 13:5
2 Corinthians 9:8
Ephesians 4:32
Philippians 3:13; 4:8
Colossians 1:27; 3:13
1 Thessalonians 5:16–18
Hebrews 12:2,14,15
1 Peter 2:21–23

Alcoholism

Psalm 9:10; 25:15; 62:5; 100:4,5
Proverbs 2:6; 14:12; 15:22; 16:16,21; 19:20,22a; 24:11,12
Matthew 19:26
Romans 14:13
2 Corinthians 1:3–5
Ephesians 4:25,29–31
Philippians 2:4; 4:11
Colossians 1:27
1 John 3:1

Anger

Genesis 4:3–8
1 Samuel 18:8
2 Samuel 12:5
1 Kings 19:4

Psalm 27:13; 34:4; 42:11; 62:5–8; 68:19; 118:8; 119:67; 139:23,24
Proverbs 15:1; 28:13
Isaiah 40:11; 41:10; 43:3,4; 48:10
Jeremiah 29:11; 31:3,4
Ezekiel 47:12
Matthew 5:23,24
John 8:32; 14:1
Romans 8:33,34; 12:2,18,19
2 Corinthians 1:4; 12:9
Ephesians 4:26
Philippians 4:13
Colossians 2:13; 3:12–14
1 Thessalonians 5:23
Hebrews 4:15,16; 12:14,15
James 1:2–4
1 Peter 1:6,7

Career Moms

Psalm 127:3
Proverbs 21:29
Romans 8:31–39
1 Corinthians 6:12; 15:57
Galatians 1:10
Ephesians 5:15–17
Philippians 4:8
Colossians 3:17,23
1 Thessalonians 5:16–18
Hebrews 13:5

Caregiving

Leviticus 19:32
Numbers 11:16,17
Psalm 62:8; 119:71
Proverbs 17:22; 18:12–13; 27:9
Matthew 20:28
Mark 6:31,32
Luke 6:31
Romans 8:9; 15:1
Galatians 6:5,9
Ephesians 6:2,3
Philippians 2:4
Colossians 3:3,13
1 Timothy 5:4,8
1 Peter 3:15; 5:14

Childlessness

Genesis 2:24
Deuteronomy 32:4
Psalm 27:13,14; 32:8; 34:18; 68:6; 119:50; 127:5
Proverbs 3:5,6; 15:22, 16:9,23; 24:26; 27:5
Isaiah 30:18,21; 43:18,19; 54:1,2
Jeremiah 29:11
Matthew 28:19,20
Romans 8:28
2 Corinthians 1:3,4
Galatians 6:2
Ephesians 1:5; 4:29; 5:22–28
1 Timothy 6:6
1 Peter 3:15

Codependency

Exodus 20:3
Psalm 51:6; 119:35
Proverbs 4:23
Isaiah 43:18,19
John 8:36
2 Corinthians 5:17
Galatians 1:10
Philippians 4:13,19
Colossians 3:13
James 2:22

Compulsive Eating

1 Samuel 16:7
Psalm 139:23,24
Proverbs 5:23; 21:2; 25:16
Romans 6
1 Corinthians 10:13,31
2 Corinthians 5:9, 10:12
Galatians 6:2
Philippians 4:8,13,19
Colossians 1:27
1 Timothy 4:8
James 1:13,14

Depression

1 Kings 19:4
Psalm 27:13; 42:11; 119:67
Isaiah 40:11; 41:10; 43:3,4; 48:10
Jeremiah 29:11
Ezekiel 47:12
John 14:1
Romans 12:2
2 Corinthians 1:4; 12:9
Hebrews 4:15,16
James 1:2–4
1 Thessalonians 5:23

Divorce

Deuteronomy 31:6
Psalm 34:18; 37; 68:5; 71:20; 139:1–16,23,24
Isaiah 43:4
Jeremiah 17:14; 29:11
Matthew 5:3–12
Romans 12:1; 13:14
1 Corinthians 6:19,20; 7:32–35
Galatians 2:20
Philippians 4:13,19
Colossians 2:9,10; 3:13
1 Thessalonians 5:18
Hebrews 4:15,16; 12:14,15
1 Peter 4:19

Dysfunctional Families

Genesis 50:20
Psalm 22:23,24
Proverbs 16:21
Ecclesiastes 3:4
Luke 9:23
Acts 5:29
Galatians 1:10
Philippians 2:13; 4:19
Colossians 1:27
Colossians 3:13
1 Thessalonians 5:18

Forgiveness

Isaiah 53:3
Matthew 18:21,22
Luke 1:37; 23:34
John 20:27
Acts 7:60
Romans 12:19
Ephesians 2:8,9; 4:32
Philippians 4:13
Colossians 3:13
1 Thessalonians 5:24
Hebrews 10:36

God's Will

Exodus 20
Deuteronomy 10:20
Psalm 32:8; 40:8

Proverbs 15:22; 24:32
Matthew 22:37
John 5:19,20; 15:5; 16:13
Romans 12:2,4–8
Ephesians 1:13,14,17,18
Philippians 2:13
1 Thessalonians 4
1 Timothy 5:8

Grief

Psalm 23:4; 30:2,5; 34:18; 100:4
2 Corinthians 1:3–5,7
Galatians 6:2
Philippians 4:11,13
Hebrews 6:19
1 John 1:9

Guilt

Psalm 32:5,8; 51:17; 103:8–12; 139:23,24
Proverbs 16:7; 28:13
Jeremiah 31:34
Matthew 5:23,24
John 16:8
Romans 8:1
2 Corinthians 7:10
Galatians 2:20
Philippians 2:13; 4:13
Colossians 1:27
Hebrews 10:10; 12:4–11
1 Peter 3:18
1 John 1:9
Revelation 12:10

Homosexuality

Psalm 27:10; 34:18; 147:3
Isaiah 43:4
Jeremiah 29:11
Ezekiel 36:26,27
Luke 4:18
John 15:5
Romans 1:26,27; 6:11–14; 12:2
1 Corinthians 6:9–11; 10:13; 15:33,34
2 Corinthians 5:17,21; 10:5
Galatians 5:1
Philippians 1:6
Hebrews 4:15; 12:1
1 Peter 2:19–23

Intimacy

Psalm 16:11
Proverbs 16:21; 18:24; 20:5
Amos 3:3
John 11:5,33–36
Romans 12:10
Philippians 2:4; 4:12,13
Colossians 1:27

Loneliness

Psalm 51:10; 62:1,8; 63:1–8, 139:23,24
Proverbs 19:22
Ecclesiastes 3:4; 4:10
John 11:35
2 Corinthians 1:3,4
Philippians 2:4; 4:19
Revelation 21:4

Mid-Life Crisis

Deuteronomy 31:8
Psalm 34:17,18
Proverbs 26:12
Isaiah 30:1
1 Peter 3:1,4

Parenting

Proverbs 13:24; 29:15
Ephesians 6:4
1 Timothy 3:4
Hebrews 12:5–13

Phobias

Deuteronomy 31:8
Psalm 23; 34:4; 46:1,2; 56:3,4; 91:2; 107:20
Proverbs 1:33; 3:25,26
Isaiah 41:10,13; 43:1
Lamentations 3:57
Zephaniah 3:15
Romans 12:2
Philippians 4:13
Colossians 1:27
2 Timothy 1:7
1 John 4:18

Premarital Pregnancy

Psalm 10:14; 25:4,5; 59:17; 68:5; 121; 138:8; 139:13–16
Isaiah 41:10; 43:18,19
Jeremiah 1:5; 29:11; 31:3
Matthew 5:44a,b
John 3:16,17; 8; 16:33
Romans 6; 12:14,19
Ephesians 4:26
Philippians 4:19
Colossians 1:27; 3:13
Hebrews 12:15
2 Peter 3:8
1 John 3:1; 4:16,18

Reconciliation

Psalm 28:7
Proverbs 6:2–3; 16:21
Joel 2:25
Matthew 18:16
Romans 8:9,28
Ephesians 3:16–19; 4:29
Philippians 2:4; 3:13,14
2 Thessalonians 3:5
James 4:17

Salvation

2 Chronicles 7:14
Matthew 16:25
Psalm 32:5; 86:5; 103:12
Proverbs 28:13
Isaiah 44:22
Jeremiah 4:16–18; 31:34; 33:8
Lamentations 3:31,32
Matthew 16:25
Mark 3:28,29
John 3:16; 10:28
Acts 3:19
Romans 3:23
Ephesians 1:4,7,13,14
Colossians 2:6
Hebrews 8:12
1 John 1:9

Self-Worth

Psalm 139
Proverbs 18:12; 19:22
Isaiah 54:10
John 15:20
Romans 15:7
1 Corinthians 13:4–8,11
2 Corinthians 5:17
Galatians 1:10
Ephesians 3:14–20
Philippians 3:12–14

Sexual Abuser

Singleness

Single Parenting

Stress

Suicide

Matthew 19:26
John 8:32; 10:11
1 Corinthians 10:13
Philippians 4:6,7

Temptation

Psalm 9:10; 50:15
Proverbs 1:7; 5:21–23; 6:27,28,32
Romans 6:11; 7:19; 8:9,13
1 Corinthians 6:18; 10:13
2 Corinthians 5:10; 12:9
Galatians 6:7,8
Philippians 4:19
1 Timothy 6:11
Titus 2:11–14
Hebrews 4:13; 13:4

Terminal Illness

Genesis 22:1–18
Deuteronomy 32:39
1 Samuel 2:6
Psalm 139:13–16
Proverbs 19:21
Ecclesiastes 3:1,2
Matthew 7:13,14; 10:31; 11:28,29
John 8:32
Romans 14:8
1 Corinthians 10:13
2 Corinthians 12:7–10
Galatians 2:20
Philippians 1:20,21
Hebrews 11:17–19
Revelation 21:4

Unbelieving Loved One

Proverbs 19:22
Isaiah 40:28
Matthew 7:7–11
Philippians 4:19
Titus 3:9
Hebrews 4:12
James 5:16
1 Peter 3:15,16

Victim Mentality

Psalm 37:10,17; 51:6; 68:19; 119:50
Proverbs 3:5,6; 12:18; 15:3
Matthew 18:15
John 3:21; 8:36
Romans 8:28; 12:2
Ephesians 4:26
Philippians 4:19
Colossians 1:27; 3:13

Wife Abuse

Psalm 11:5; 13
Proverbs 19:19
John 8:32
Romans 13:1–3,5
1 Corinthians 7:10,11
Galatians 1:10
Colossians 3:13